CLASSIC GUNS OF THE WORLD SERIES

WALTHER P.38

GERMANY'S 9 MM SEMIAUTOMATIC
PISTOL IN WORLD WAR II

WALTHER P.38

GERMANY'S 9 MM SEMIAUTOMATIC
PISTOL IN WORLD WAR II

STÉPHANE CAILLEAU

CLASSIC GUNS OF THE WORLD SERIES

WALTHER P.38

MARKINGS

AMMUNITION

ACCESSORIES

MILITARY

4880 Lower Valley Road ■ Atglen, PA 19310

Originally published as *Le P.38: Le successeur du Luger*
by RÉGI Arm, Paris © 1999, RÉGI Arm
Translated from the French by Julia and Frédéric Finel
Library of Congress Control Number: 2019947654

Cover design by Justin Watkinson
Type set in Helvetica Neue LT Pro/Times New Roman

ISBN: 978-0-7643-5967-5
Printed in China

Published by Schiffer Publishing, Ltd.
4880 Lower Valley Road
Atglen, PA 19310
Phone: (610) 593-1777; Fax: (610) 593-2002
E-mail: Info@schifferbooks.com
Web: www.schifferbooks.com

For our complete selection of fine books on this and related subjects,
please visit our website at www.schifferbooks.com.
You may also write for a free catalog.

Schiffer Publishing's titles are available at special discounts for
bulk purchases for sales promotions or premiums. Special editions,
including personalized covers, corporate imprints, and excerpts,
can be created in large quantities for special needs.
For more information, contact the publisher.

We are always looking for people to write books on new
and related subjects. If you have an idea for a book,
please contact us at proposals@schifferbooks.com.

CONTENTS

CHAPTER 1

HISTORY

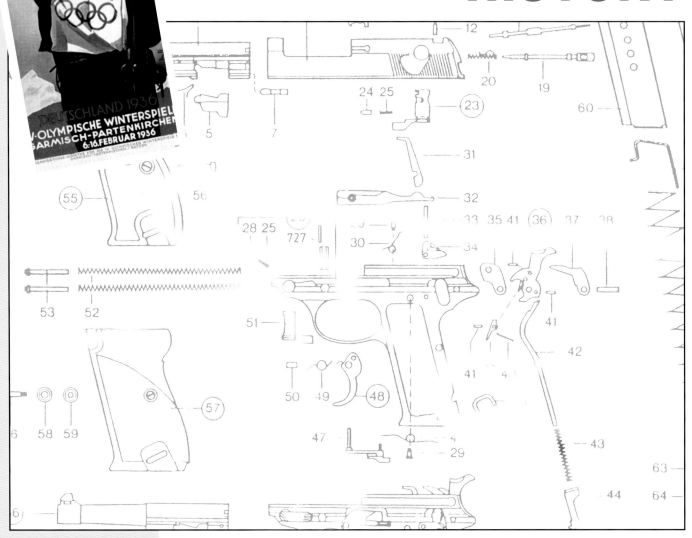

Top: A Walther PP civilian pistol (aluminum frame); **bottom**, a Walther PPK marked RZM placed on an illustrated album of the Berlin Olympic Games. A box of twenty-five 7.65 mm cartridges completes the picture.

AT THE END OF THE SIXTEENTH CENTURY, THE SMALL TOWNS OF ZELLA AND MEHLIS, IN THURINGE, WERE RENOWNED FOR THEIR TRADITION IN WEAPONS MAKING.

In 1886, a certain Carl Walther (born in 1860) set up a store that specialized in the sale of weapons in Zella-Mehlis. It was a modest family enterprise that made hunting rifles and small defense pistols. At that time the concept of the (semi)automatic pistol was slowly taking shape with the development of the Borchardt (and Borchardt-Luger) system and the Mauser C96.

Between 1908 and 1921, the Carl Walther Waffenfabrik expanded and conceived a series of semiautomatic pistols chambered in 6.35 mm and 7.65 mm caliber. They were commonly named as models 1, 2, 3, and so on (up to model 9). These pistols had a glorious commercial success at a time when competition in this area was particularly severe (John M. Browning already had a prominent place in the market). Only the model 6 was the object of a modest military contract during the First World War. The patriarch, Carl Walther, died in 1915, and his three sons took over the reins at the head of the company. It was more particularly Fritz Walther who took care of weapons design, while Georg and Erich took care of the administrative and commercial side of the company.

Under the leadership of Fritz Walther, automatic rifles, sports weapons, flare pistols, and even compressed-air guns and starting guns came out of the company workshops.

Concerning specifically the domain of competition weapons, the Zella-Mehlis company designed sports pistol model 1926

(renamed Olympia model 32 for the Los Angeles Olympic Games of 1932) and Olympia model 36, with which the German competitors in the Berlin Olympics won six medals. These pistols are chambered in .22 short caliber and .22 long rifle. Different versions of these excellent pistols (sometimes improved with a counterweight) are also proposed to sports shooters in Europe and in the United States.

The design and commercialization of the Walther PP (in 1929) and Walther PPK (in 1931) contributed to establish the reputation of the Walther company once and for all. The development of a reliable double-action trigger revolutionized the world of the handgun; these pistols, with a timeless appearance, represented success on an international scale, and many political and military organizations of Nazi Germany were equipped with them. Their design was based on 7.65 mm caliber, and they were also produced in 6.35 mm, 9 mm short, and .22 long-rifle caliber.

From the beginning of the 1930s, the Carl Walther Waffenfabrik tried hard to develop a modern hand weapon, chambered in 9 mm Parabellum caliber. The clear objective of this research was to clinch a large military contract. Different prototypes, conceived with the collaboration of a company engineer named Fritz Barthelmes, were formulated to this end, and these were different MP (Militär Pistole) and AP (Armee Pistole). At this stage they already unequivocally brought to mind what the future P.38 would look like, in terms both of its external appearance and its mechanism. This long task eventually resulted in the realization of the HP model (Heeres Pistole or literally army pistol), which had a certain amount of success on the commercial market.

In 1937, the OKH (Oberkommando des Heeres of the German Military High Command) approached a series of arms producers with a view to adopting a new regulation pistol.

Handgun training at the shooting range (from the *Olympia* album, 1936)

Poster of the Berlin Olympic Games of 1936

A forerunner: the Walther AP model (army pistol) shown with some period factory documents

P.38 DIMENSIONS	
Weight	900 g (empty magazine)
	Approx. 1,050 g with an eight-round magazine
Total length	215 mm
Thickness	37 mm
Height	137 mm

Artillery officer equipped with a PP pistol in a leather holster. *ECPA*

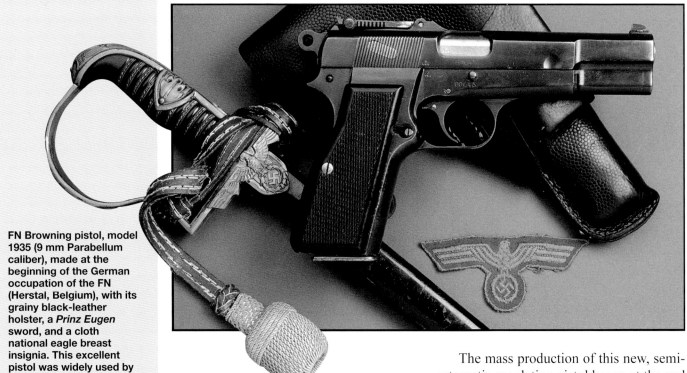

FN Browning pistol, model 1935 (9 mm Parabellum caliber), made at the beginning of the German occupation of the FN (Herstal, Belgium), with its grainy black-leather holster, a *Prinz Eugen* sword, and a cloth national eagle breast insignia. This excellent pistol was widely used by the Waffen-SS.

A fine example of "coexistence in the field" of the P.38 (carried by the soldier on the left) and the P.08 (*at right*). *ECPA*

The wishes of the OKH were simple and logical: a semiautomatic pistol in 9 mm Parabellum caliber that was easy to disassemble, with perfectly interchangeable parts and with as few parts as possible.

In addition to Walther, which proposed its HP model, there were three other manufacturers in competition: Mauser, with the model HSv; Sauer & Sohn; and (possibly) Berlinsuhler Waffen & Fahizeugwerke. The HP model was the favorite and came in an easy first place. After several new and minor mechanical modifications, the choice of pistol was approved in 1938, and it then received the name P.38 ("P" for Pistol and 38 for the year 1938).

The mass production of this new, semi-automatic regulation pistol began at the end of 1939. It concerned the first P.38 to carry the military inspection stamp (eagle/359), which makes up part of the zero series. The P.38 pistol was officially adopted on April 26, 1940.

PRODUCTION

When specialist literature on the subject is consulted, it becomes clear that the figures concerning P.38 production are controversial. Different authors, the majority of whom are English speaking, have dealt with this difficult subject, and after comparison it appears that these estimations, coming from varying sources and methods of evaluation, have a narrow margin fluctuating between 5 and 10 percent. Considering the absence of "more precise" original documents, it makes sense to be satisfied with this small margin of error. With that in mind, we arrive at a total production figure fluctuating between 1,186,000 and 1,250,000 (military) P.38s made between 1939 and 1945.

The quantity breakdown by manufacturer is as follows:

- Walther: 574,000 to 583,000

- Spreewerke: 283,000 to 304,000

- Mauser: 329,000 to 369,000

On the other hand, there is no doubt that the P.38 was the most used semiautomatic German pistol during the last world conflict. Statistically

it pushed the P.08 into second place toward the end of 1944. The reader should be aware that there can be a difference between total production figures and the number of specimens distributed to the armed forces.

These estimations merely serve as a guide to the collector doing research. It is evident that a P.38, of which 7,200 were made (such as the Walther code "480"), is theoretically much more difficult to acquire than a "byf43," of which more than 162,000 specimens were made. It is also necessary to consider geographical differences in the allocation of the P.38 of the Nazi period. It is noted that of the examples at the end of the war, type "ac45" or "svw45" is more common in the United States than in Europe, whereas the Walthers of the early 1940s are slightly more frequent in Europe. This state of affairs is connected with the liberation of a good part of Europe and the occupation of Nazi Germany by hundreds of thousands of US combatants, who appreciated, with justification, this type of "bulky souvenir" and took the opportunity to bring back these trophies without running the risk of breaking the law. In addition, after the war, entire batches of pistols were bought by intermediaries and resold on the North American continent. More recently, the disappearance of the Eastern Bloc allowed for new trade deals, with the arrival of a considerable number of P.38s (among others) from some of these countries (Ukraine, for example). It was for all these reasons that the P.38, along with many German handguns, is very well represented in North America.

The German armed forces were equipped with the P.38 along with a certain number of handguns chambered in 9 mm Parabellum. Apart from the essential P.08 (commonly known as the Luger), the Oberkommando der Wehrmacht obtained different semiautomatic pistols of the same caliber during the Second World War. This was how occupied countries such as Poland and Belgium participated and supplied the VIS M1935 and the FN Browning model 1935, respectively. The intrinsic qualities of these pistols were not missed by German military leaders. They put the requisitioned back into operation on behalf of their own armed forces. In the south of Europe, the Germans traded with Franco's Spain, which, even though officially neutral, handed over Star pistols such as model B and Astra 600, among others.

For those interested in figures, it is estimated that the German army obtained just over 2,400,000 handguns between 1934 and 1945. The most-common calibers were 9 mm Parabellum and 7.65 mm. The principal (German) manufacturers of these handguns were Mauser, Walther, Spreewerke, and Sauer & Sohn. The division of these weapons between the different branches of the German army was in broad terms carried out in the following manner: 66 percent for the Heer (army) and the Waffen-SS, 25 percent for the Luftwaffe (air force), and 6 percent for the Kriegsmarine (navy).

DESCRIPTION, OPERATION, AND DISASSEMBLY

DESCRIPTION

The P.38 is composed of four main parts:

- barrel (and its retainer latch)

- breech block (or slide)

- frame

- magazine

The barrel of the P.38 is typically clear and extends 6.4 cm from the end of the slide, giving this pistol its eminently characteristic appearance. At its extremity, it has a triangular-shaped foresight, which can be moved to the left or the right in order to optimize accuracy. Occasionally the number 1, 2, or 3 can be found on its side; these figures correspond to the different sizes of the foresight. From 1943, the numbers 4 and 5 were added, following on from the use of new ammunition. The barrel has six grooves on the right. The diameter of this barrel (8.5, for example) was engraved on the inner side (until end of 1941). The locking bolt is closely linked with the lower part of the barrel, which is distinguishable by the absence of bronzing.

The slide, machined from a solid block of steel, shows the upper part of the barrel. It has a series of ridges on its external lateral lining that facilitate arming. A nonadjustable, U-shaped backsight occupies the rear part of this slide. On some HP models and other early P.38 models (notably, the zero series), the gunsights were occasionally painted in red and black. This sighting

The four main elements of a P.38: the barrel with retainer latch, slide, frame, and the magazine

notch blocks the cover of the slide, which gives access to the firing pin and the loaded-chamber indicator pin. The latter protrudes approximately 4 mm at the rear of the slide (above the external hammer) when a cartridge occupies the chamber. By looking at it (in daylight) or feeling it (in the dark), the shooter can gauge the state of preparation of his P.38. Note also the presence of an external extractor on the left lateral surface of the slide. The first HP models, as well as the P.38 in the zero series (first subvariant only), still have an internal extractor. The safety lever is positioned level with the left lateral ridges of this slide. This manual safety is similar to that on the Walther PP and PPK. The safety is activated when the lever is lowered and the letter "S," painted in white, appears. The "S" means *Sicherheit* in German (in English, "safety"). In the upper position the safety lever shows the letter "F" in red (for *Feuer* in German or "fire" in English). The P.38 is also equipped with an empty magazine safety, which keeps the bolt open when the magazine is empty. On the other hand, it does not have a magazine safety, meaning in the event of losing the magazine, it is possible to operate with single-shot fire. The last safety mechanism is none other than the brought-down safety, which prevents any accidental maneuvering of the firing pin.

The frame exposes two powerful recoil springs on both sides of the rear part, which store energy when the slide moves back. It also presents the locking bolt on the forward part of the left side. As its name indicates, this lever allows the separation of the frame from the barrel-slide group. The slide stop is near this lever and is also positioned on the left side of the frame. The wide trigger guard allowed firing while the user was wearing gloves. Also present on the frame is a small receptacle in which the bolt falls during the short backward movement of the barrel. On the right side of the frame there is a pin that transfers the pressure on the trigger through the hammer mechanism. There are two grips in Bakelite, plastic, wood, or even metal. They are joined with the frame by way of a long screw, the head of which is turned toward the left, and they cover the trigger mechanism. There is a lanyard loop on the left lower part of the frame. The magazine release catch is situated on the lower part of the grip. It must be pushed toward the rear to allow the magazine to be introduced or removed.

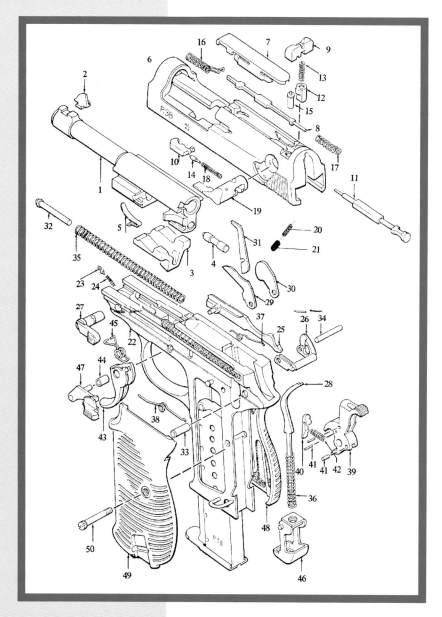

An inquiry into the use of the P.38 given to some regiments in 1940

OPERATION

As far as the mode of operation is concerned, it is normally said that the P.38 is operated by short recoil of the barrel. When the shot is fired, the barrel slide group moves back by about 7 mm. At that point, the locking bolt is forced to swing downward through contact with a lever, which makes it protrude, meaning the barrel rear movement is stopped. Only the slide can continue with its rearward movement, bringing about the extraction of the case, the rearming of the hammer, and the compression of both recoil springs. It is the springs that produce the forward return of the slide and the introduction of a new cartridge in the chamber. At the end of this forward movement, the slide retrieves the locking bolt (and the barrel) on its way enabling it to move back up and lock.

The main characteristic of this pistol is the possibility of double-action fire, meaning that firing is possible when the hammer is at rest by simply pressing on the trigger. This principle allows the shooter to carry a loaded (i.e., with a bullet in the chamber) weapon, but "on safe" (i.e., with the hammer lowered). If necessary, the weapon is still ready to fire, since it is sufficient to press on the trigger, which will arm the hammer and then press on the firing pin. This design gave it an undeniable advantage for a weapon of war.

DISASSEMBLY

Basic disassembly of the P.38 is in fact very simple. After carrying out the usual checks concerning the absence of ammunition in the weapon, pull the slide back by holding it with the slide grips until it reaches the slide stop. Remove the magazine from its housing and swing down the barrel latch frontward. Now the slide, solid with the barrel, can be moved forward by lowering the hammer and the slide stop. Move the slide-barrel group forward and separate it from the frame. Pull down on the locking piece to easily separate the barrel from the slide. To remove the grips, take out the screws that fix the grips to the frame. Basic stripping is now complete, giving the main parts of the P.38 (namely, the frame, slide, barrel, and its locking bolt). These parts can now be cleaned and oiled in the usual way. The amateur who wishes to take things further can undertake the disassembly of the slide by removing the cover. This maneuver means that the rear sight, firing-pin lock, and firing-pin block can be removed.

The loaded-chamber indicator is removed from the front, the firing pin from the rear, and the firing-pin spring from the top. Disassembly of the rest of the frame is necessary only on rare occasions and will not be detailed here.

For the reassembly of the P.38, the reverse order is followed; the locking bolt must be in up position so that the slide barrel group can be put back on the frame, using the grooves, and moved backward. It is often necessary to lower the small parts (ejector, firing-pin lock lifter) that jut out during movement of the slide barrel group. Then the barrel latch can be moved back and the barrel slide can move into position.

Weapon diagram

DISASSEMBLING THE P.38

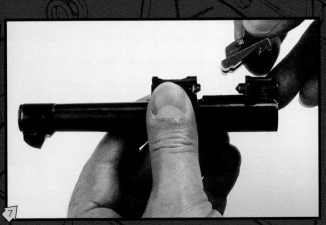

1. Pull the slide back, holding the slide grips.

2. Remove the magazine.

3. Turn the slide lock forward.

4. Lower the slide stop.

5. After moving back the hammer, move the slide-barrel unit forward.

6. Press the locking block button (operating pin) to separate the barrel from the breech block.

7. Remove the locking block by turning it forward.

The famous logo of
the Walther company

The code "480," used
briefly by the Walther
company in 1940

The code "ac" attributed
to Walther, above
the figure 41 (for
the year 1941)

The code "cyq" attributed
to the Spreewerke factory:
note the absence of
the date

The code "byf" used
by the Mauser factory,
above the figure 44
(for the year 1944)

The code "svw" attributed
to Mauser in 1945

A Sd.Kfz.231 in the
south of France, 1942.
Bundesarchiv

IDENTIFICATION AND CLASSIFICATION

In order to correctly identify a P.38, the following information must be considered:

1. The manufacturer's name or code

This very important mark appears on the left side of the slide. Only the initial production by Walther bore the name of the manufacturer in the shape of the famous Walther banner; this was for P.38s from the zero series. Subsequently, all the P.38s assembled by Walther along with the two other contracting parties bear a manufacturer's code. The purpose of these codes was to hide the origin of the weapons (and other armaments) from the enemy.

In this context, Walther applied two successive codes: first, the code "480," which was used temporarily, followed by the code "ac," which was much more common. This code "ac" can, however, as an exception, be found on P.38s coming from the workshops of the two other contractors. Spreewerke used the code "cyq" (and the code "cvq"). Mauser used the code "byf" when it first began assembling the P.38. It ended the war with the code "svw."

2. The year of manufacture

This is closely associated with the manufacturer's code and is composed of the last two figures of whatever the current year was. The figures are placed either under or just after the code. There is a major exception to this rule: Spreewerke never specified the year of manufacture of its P.38s. Walther printed this date only from the end of 1940.

3. The serial number

This has from one to four figures, from 1 to 9999. A minuscule letter is often associated as a suffix and, less commonly, as a prefix. The serial number is visible on the left side of the slide, the base of the barrel, the left side of the frame, and the locking bolt (reminder of the last three figures and the letter). With very rare exceptions*, the serial numbers found on the P.38 (as was the case for all German weapons of that time) must match. When this was not the case, there was no doubt that it was the result of a reassembly from parts from other P.38s.

Consequently, to identify a P.38, the manufacturer's code, the year of manufacture, the serial number, and the accompanying letter must be known; for example, a P.38 code "ac44," bearing the serial number 3706b. In proceeding this way, it is certain that no two P.38s will have the same number. A more detailed identification would entail an analysis of the different inspection stamps, which are discussed in the following paragraph. The HP models present a series of small differences in relation to the rules mentioned here. These particular cases are detailed in the following chapter.

Regarding the classification of the different P.38 types, it must be recognized that they respond essentially to the will of the collectors rather than the reality of the time. The proposed variants and subvariants are based on the presence or absence of certain markings and also on the features of the finish. In spite of its artificial and arbitrary nature, this type of classification is nonetheless very useful since it allows collectors (and others interested in the subject) to speak the same language. When, for example, a collector in Atlanta, Paris, or Brussels talks about a first subvariant of a P.38 "ac41," everyone knows what is being referred to.**

* Such as, for example, inversions of the figures 6 and 9 or possible mistakes in the stamping process or oversights, as well as some end-of-war assemblies and other reassemblies in the arsenal

** In order to improve the legibility of the different markings that are present, they were treated (by the current owner) with white India ink. Its application is extremely simple and requires only the possible layer of protective oil to be removed. This product has no risk for the bronzing or the adjacent metal. In addition, it can easily be removed with a damp cloth. Originally there were only the letters "S" and "F," relating to the safety system, which were painted in white and red.

An extremely rare one-figure serial number

Two-figure serial number

Three-figure serial number

The most common four-figure serial number

INSPECTION STAMPS

The amateur collector of German regulation weapons is inevitably confronted with different stamps applied on this type of material. In this context the following points must be stated.

1. Military test marks

They prove only that the marked weapon has been tested with a cartridge containing an "excessive" charge of powder and that it can, consequently, be used in "complete safety" with standard ammunition. All parts of the weapon likely to be affected by this excess pressure are marked.

Concerning more specifically the P.38, there are three components that benefit from this marking: the slide (on the right side), the barrel, and the locking bolt. This task of inspection, carried out in the factory, even fell on the shoulders of civilian inspectors. They were responsible for their work regarding the Wehrmacht through the HeereswaffenAmt.

Three types of markings followed during the period from 1934 to 1945, but the only one applied on the P.38 was none other than a small stylized eagle with deployed wings bearing a swastika in its claws (eagle/swastika as an abbreviation).

2. Military inspection stamps

These indicate that the component of a marked weapon was produced according to specific prescriptions and to a sufficient standard so as to be used by different branches of the armed forces. The presence of this stamp proves only that the component of the P.38 has passed tests required for military use. These stamps have evolved a lot over the years and have therefore known different designs: a single number, a number on top of an eagle, or a number on a stylized eagle carrying a swastika. Several theories circulated about the significance of the numbers accompanying these famous birds. It seems that the figures corresponded to either a specific bureau or inspector responsible for the mission.

Military inspection stamps are found on all types of equipment such as shells, grenades, machine guns, magazine loaders, and so on. As many as 25,000 inspectors were counted (in 1941), who reported to fourteen regional offices. The superior officer heading each office was responsible to the HeereswaffenAmt.

Very probably an original reassembly of an unnumbered Spreewerke barrel (eagle/88) on a Walther-made P.38 (code "ac42," eagle/359)

Heer soldier equipped with a P.38 pistol

Military test mark (eagle/swastika)

Military inspection stamps on weapons from the Walther factory (eagle/359)

Military inspection stamps on weapons from the Spreewerke factory (eagle/88)

Military inspection stamps on weapons from the Mauser factory (eagle/135)

Military inspection stamps on weapons from the Mauser factory (eagle/WaA135)

Military inspection stamps on weapons from the DWM Werk (eagle/WaA140)

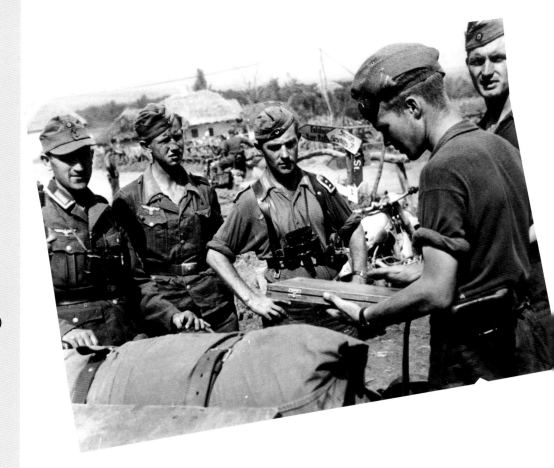

Commercial test mark (eagle/N)

The true Military Armament Office situated in Berlin organized the supply of weapons to all branches of the German army. The letters "WaA" were the abbreviation of the WaffenAmt and were very often included in the stamp.

It should be noted that there were also specific inspection systems for certain material destined for the Luftwaffe and the Kriegsmarine.

3. Commercial test marks

These marks are the counterpart of the military test marks applied on weapons destined for the commercial sector. After September 1939 the inspectors involved simultaneously took part in tests for weapons destined for the armed forces.

In the case of the P.38 the stamps concerned only some HP models and the P.38 of the police. There are two types:

- a capital "N" on a crown (abbreviated to crown/N), used between 1891 and April 1940

- a capital "N" on a stylized eagle (abbreviated to eagle/N), applied from April 1940 onward

4. Police inspection stamps

The recognition of these different stamps proves to be extremely useful during the examination of weapons and German military equipment dating from that period. In practice, these markings are "unavoidable" for the collector, and as such it is indispensable to be able to interpret them correctly.

WALTHER

A Walther model P.38 with a small instruction manual dated 1940 (serial number 10751)

In a context of latent remilitarization, the Carl Walther Waffenfabrik produced a series of semiautomatic pistols in the thirties that can logically be considered as the precursors to the P.38. They have a certain number of features in common:

- finished to a very high degree

- a very small number of assembled specimens

- double action (with very rare exceptions)

- the 9 mm Parabellum caliber, but also versions in .45 and 7.65 mm caliber

- artisanal manufacture giving rise to small differences in measurements

- weapons initially not destined for the commercial sector

- the logo of the Walther firm on the left side of the slide

PRECURSORS

Proceeding chronologically, it is acknowledged that the first of these prototypes was named the model MP-PP (Militär Pistole-PP). Fresh from the commercial success of its double-action trigger, the Zella-Mehlis firm conceived an oversized hybrid of the Walther PP chambered in 9 mm Parabellum caliber. It was operated by single recoil of the barrel and had an apparent external hammer. Five specimens of this "ancestor" were identified.

After having conceived a first MP (Militär Pistole) model with external hollowed hammer (of which there is only one specimen), which also is operated by a single recoil of the barrel, Walther tackled the program of MP and AP models with nonapparent hammer. This research program accompanied the significant changes in design as well as in the operation of these weapons. The following are distinguished within this series of prototypes:

1. The MP first model (with hidden hammer) was manufactured between 1932 and 1934. This is a single part that functions in the same way as its direct predecessor. The rear part of the slide projects above the frame and thus hides the hammer. The barrel protrudes completely due to the absence of the junction of the slide above the barrel. Two longitudinal guideways on either side of the slide reinforce the mechanical structure. The locking bolt and the slide stop are positioned on the

Carl and Fritz Walther

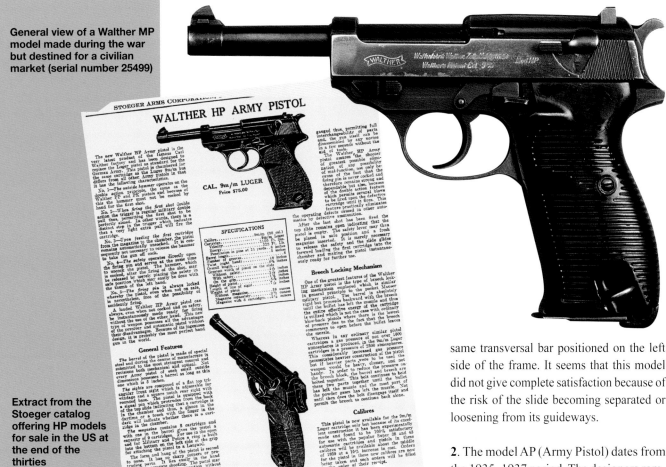

General view of a Walther MP model made during the war but destined for a civilian market (serial number 25499)

Extract from the Stoeger catalog offering HP models for sale in the US at the end of the thirties

same transversal bar positioned on the left side of the frame. It seems that this model did not give complete satisfaction because of the risk of the slide becoming separated or loosening from its guideways.

2. The model AP (Army Pistol) dates from the 1935–1937 period. The designers remedied the flaws of the previous model by placing a junction of the slide above the barrel. In this way a single lateral guideway on each side was deemed to be necessary. The famous locking block made its first appearance. It is noted also that the locking bolt and the slide stop separate into two distinct structures. The hammer and the extractor are not apparent. The estimation concerning total production of these AP models is between 50 and 200 specimens. Some lightened variants in aluminum, stock holsters, and barrels of different lengths were all tested in this series.

3. The second model MP was conceived in the mid-thirties. On the outside it slightly resembles a first model of MP, on which the two lateral guideways were removed. The lateral sides of the frame were therefore flat in the manner of those on the future P.38. The locking bolt and the slide stop remain distinct, and their manufacture was simplified. The presence of a loaded chamber indicator should be noted. This model does not stand out because of its astronomical production numbers, since only three specimens of this variant were officially indexed. This second model MP ended the series of Walther with nonapparent hammer.

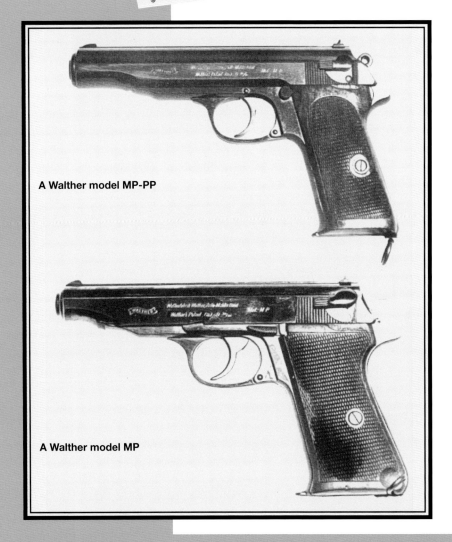

A Walther model MP-PP

A Walther model MP

In 1936 and 1937, Walther made an MP model with apparent hammer that represented the last specimen of the MP family. Apart from the modifications of the slide and the frame designed to accommodate an external hammer, this final representative of a "long line" of the MP keeps the same method of operation and the same appearance as the second model of MP. It has a loaded-chamber indicator, a firing pin with a rectangular cross section, and a rounded external hammer. Only the 9 mm Parabellum caliber seems to have been used. It is rightly considered as the direct predecessor of the HP model and the future P.38.

The Walther model HP (Heeres Pistole) was developed in 1937 and was produced on a small scale throughout the following years. It is found in different calibers, with the 9 mm Parabellum and the 7.65 mm being the most represented calibers (ahead of the .45 and the .38 super). These pistols all benefited from a very high degree of finish in the form of a superb glossy blue bronzing applied by Walther at that time. Within the HP series, it was clear that a certain number of modifications were to follow. The internal extractor adopted an external position, giving it a greater solidity. The shape of the firing pin was also modified: from a rectangular cross section, it became round. A small number of these pistols were assembled with aluminum frames, the objective being the desire for a weapon that was lighter but more solid and reliable. It was therefore the model HP, the result of long years of research, that the Walther company proposed to OKH during tests set up to determine the potential replacement of the P.08.

To sum up, it can be stated that the Zella-Mehlis firm put all its knowledge and ingenuity into the elaboration of a semiautomatic pistol chambered in 9 mm Parabellum caliber liable to be adopted by the German army. Even the denominations attributed to these predecessors went all out to appeal to the military decision makers: army pistol, military pistol, land army pistol; it is difficult to be more explicit than that. But leaving semantics to one side, OKH adopted this highly effective pistol in 1938 under the name P.38.

In the months following the green light from OKW, Walther began producing its first "military" P.38. Walther referred to them by the term "zero series."

ZERO SERIES

This particular denomination comes from the fact that the serial number of these P.38s is preceded by the figure zero. In reality, it was a P.38 that was part of a test series. Between the end of 1939 and mid-1940, it is estimated that 10,000 to 13,000 specimens of all the first regulation models would come out of the Zella-Mehlis company workshops.

Invoice from the Walther company dated October 20, 1941, to the administrative department from the Luftwaffe for the delivery of 9 mm P.38, and the PPK in 7.65 mm

During the Russian campaign, a PzKpfw.V "Panther," with a soldier carrying cases of cartridge belts

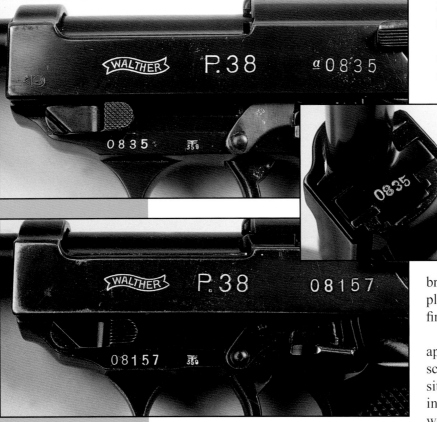

Markings on the left side of a zero series P.38 (first subvariant) bearing the serial number a0835

Serial number applied on the base of the barrel

Markings on the left side of a P.38 of the third subvariant of the zero series (serial number 08157)

3. The third subvariant gathers together specimens with numbers between 3501 and 13000. Apart from the presence of an external extractor, there is a firing pin with a round cross section.

These structural and operational modifications support the fact that all these P.38s were part of an experimental series, designed to be modified if need be.

The finish of these regulation pistols is exceptional. Walther applied a very high-quality bronzing on the zero series P.38. It was a very uniform, blue-black, glossy bronzing applied on a metal that was completely free of any trace of machining. This finish remained in use until mid-1941.

The grips are made in black plastic. Their appearance was highly reminiscent of "fish scales." The holder used to attach the lanyard, situated at the base of the left grip, was oval in shape. The grips were struck with the weapon number on the inner side. The zero series did not have exclusivity on these types of grips, since they are occasionally found on other P.38s made in 1940 and even 1941 (codes "ac40" and "ac41"). Conversely, some of the last examples of zero series (that is to say, essentially specimens of the third subvariant) are provided with "normal" grips in Bakelite, with horizontal grooves.

The famous Walther banner marking is found on the left side of the slide. This small banner represents the principal feature, in terms of markings, of the three subvariants of the P.38. From this, the P.38 initials followed by the serial number can be seen. The stamping is clear and uniform. This serial number is repeated on the left side of the frame, level with the front of the trigger guard, under the barrel (on the forward part of the base of the barrel), and also on the locking bolt (a repeat of the last three figures).

The military inspection stamps (eagle/359) are dispersed on the main parts of the weapon: a stamp on the left side of the frame, two others on the right side of the slide, and one on the barrel and the locking bolt. The WaffenAmt stamp is also applied on what are commonly known as "small parts"; in other words, the trigger, hammer, slide cover, slide stop, disassembly tool, and so on. As for the military test marks of eagle and swastika, they are on the right side of

Various authors distinguish three subvariants of the P.38 zero series:

1. The first subvariant includes the first 1,000 P.38s assembled. They are characterized by the presence of a firing pin of rectangular cross section and an internal extractor.

2. The second subvariant includes the serial numbers between 1001 and 3500. The firing pin has a rectangular cross section, but the extractor adopts an internal position.

The plastic grips known as "fish scale"

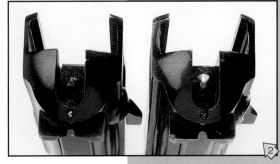

the breech block (surrounded by two eagles/359), as well as on the barrel and the locking block.

The Walther zero series has other particularities:

1. Some of them have a minuscule letter as a suffix or prefix, which essentially figure on the frame and the breech block (together or separately). The letter in question can be underlined. The exact meaning of these letters is not known; however, several hypotheses have been put forward on this subject:

• Two parts were made with the same number; the addition of a letter differentiates them.

• The letter corresponds to a part of the weapon that has been tested, then integrated into a fully completed weapon.

Whatever the case, only a small number (fewer than a dozen) of these P.38s were indexed with these letters. They can be found in each one of the three subvariants.

2. Some WaffenAmt stamps, applied on the breech blocks, the frames, or both, appear to have been stamped in an incomplete way. The stylized eagle is missing one part of its wing and could therefore correspond to an eagle/AaA359 stamp (rather than eagle/359). Here again the reason for this is not known.

Also noteworthy is the fact that a very small number of the very first specimens bear a reminder of the last two figures of the serial number on the small parts (as on the P.08).

3. Occasionally, unique (or nearly so) variations within the same three subvariants can be found. This illustrates the multiple attempts to improve the operation of the P.38, which became regulation in the German army. Some of these modifications were not pursued but are the source of interest among P.38 collectors more than seventy years later. These modifications can theoretically concern all the components of the pistol.

The prototype, with its remarkable finish, lent the zero series P.38 an almost mythical status. It goes without saying that the parts are the first choice for the amateur collector.

1. Comparison of the extractors: internal extractor on the left (first subvariant) and external extractor on the right (second subvariant)

2. Comparison of the firing pins: rectangular section firing pin on the left and circular section on the right

3. Comparison of slides: *on the left,* an example of the first subvariant; *on the right,* an example of the third subvariant

Details of stamps: two military inspection stamps (eagle/359) surrounding a military test stamp (eagle/swastika)

The sergeant leading this column is holding a P.38, recognizable by its distinctive outline. The infantryman behind has fixed his bayonet on his 98k rifle. *ECPA*

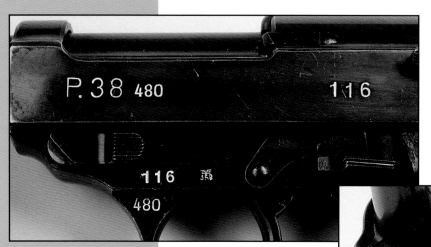

Markings present on the left side of a P.38 bearing the code "480" (serial number 116)

Serial number on the base of the barrel

Detail of the markings on a very rare P.38 "ac" without date

Opposite page: A Walther-made P.38 (code "ac44," serial number 943k) is associated with a belt with its Wehrmacht buckle, a bayonet model 1884/98 for the 98k rifle, a Russian front medal, the Infantry Assault badge (Infanterie-Sturmabzeichen), and two boxes of cartridges of 9 mm Parabellum (code "aux," year 42).

CODE "480"

The famous Walther banner was replaced by a three-figure code: "480." The first code used by Walther seems to have been attributed to it from 1934, but for reasons that are not entirely clear, it was applied on pistols only between mid-1940 and October 1940.

Production of these P.38 code "480" pistols is estimated at 7,200 specimens. The serial numbers go from 1 to 7200 (consequently there is never a letter suffix).

The finish is very top of the range, even though these P.38s represent the first standard production models. The mounted grips are mostly standard, striated, and in Bakelite, which appear on the last specimens of the zero series. But it is not unusual to come across some P.38s of this series with "fish scale" plastic grips. This "480" figure code is sometimes found stamped on the inside of the grips. This feature was also present on zero series P.38 grips or some HP models.

The code "480" is therefore found just below the P.38 initials on the left side of the breech block. It is repeated on the forward part of the trigger guard on the left side. The serial number of the weapon is on the slide, just forward of the safety lever, on the frame level with the forward part of the trigger guard, and under the base of the barrel. The grips are also numbered. The locking block has the last three figures. The standard military inspection stamps (eagle/359) are distributed on the main components of the pistol (i.e., the frame, the breech block, the barrel, and the locking bolt) and on numerous "small parts" (hammer, trigger). The military test marks (eagle/swastika) are found on the right side of the breech block, framed by two eagles/359, as well as on the barrel and the locking bolt.

As a curiosity, it should be pointed out that two P.38 examples (code "480") were discovered with the figure "40" added. The highly temporary nature of this code coupled with the exceptional finish of these code "480" P.38s makes these weapons much appreciated among connoisseurs.

THE "AC" CODE WITHOUT A DATE

In October 1940, the Zella-Mehlis firm changed their code again. It introduced at that time the code "ac," which it would keep until the end of hostilities. This code was applied, initially, without making reference to the date of manufacture. Total production of these "'ac' orphans" stands at only 2,800.

The serial numbers continue on from those used for the "480" series and consequently range from 7201 and 9800. It can be deduced that there was never a letter as a suffix on the "ac" P.38 without a date.

Concerning markings, the initials P.38 are found at the end of the left side of the breech block, followed by the letters "ac" and finally the serial number next to the safety lever. The serial number is repeated on the left side of the frame, the barrel, and the locking bolt (in the form of a repetition of the last three figures). This "ac" code is also repeated on the forward part of the trigger guard and on the left side of the frame, but not under the barrel. The military test marks (eagle/swastika) are applied on the right side of the slide, the barrel, and the locking bolt. The military inspection stamps (eagle/359) are distributed over the left side of the frame, the right side of the breech block (in duplicate), the barrel, the locking bolt, and the numerous small parts. The finish of these pistols remains excellent. The grips are of a standard type in black Bakelite.

The main attraction of this marking comes from the fact that it corresponds to the first appearance of the code "ac" on a P.38 and is also one of the rarest military variants.

CODE "AC40"

Considering the previous comments, it could easily be deduced that the P.38s bearing the "ac40" code all were assembled during the months of November and December 1940. Despite the relatively short period of time, it

This German army corporal is shown on his BMW motorcycle. He has a fine first-model holster on his left hip.

Details of markings on an "ac40" added

Repeat of the serial number on the base of the barrel

Markings on a standard "ac40" bearing the serial number 6505b

Magazine with the same number as the weapon

trigger guard and also under the barrel. Last, the military inspection stamps (type eagle/359) are on the left side of the frame, the right side of the breech block (in duplicate), the barrel, and the locking bolt. The small parts are still tested individually. The military test markings (type eagle/swastika) are present at the three points previously mentioned.

is possible to distinguish two subvariants of the code "ac40":

1. The first is called "ac40" added. It in fact concerns pistols on which the figure "40" was applied after the weapon had been completed. It would appear that the "40" was engraved by the pantographic technique, after the weapon had been bronzed. When it is examined closely, it is clear that the figure "4" is of a smaller size and is "closed." Numerous minuscule concentric circles formed by the rotation of the point of the tool can be seen. The number of specimens assembled for this category of P.38 is estimated to be 5,700. The numbering concerning this model goes from 9988 to the end of the letter "a." Concerning markings, the code "ac" can be found at the level of the

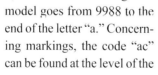

2. The second subvariant is none other than the standard "ac40" model. In this case, the "40" is applied in the usual way, meaning at the same time as the other markings and before the bronzing process. The morphology of this "40" is consequently slightly different in terms of color (blue), size (larger), and shape (open). The production of these "ac40" standard is estimated at 12,400 specimens. The range is spread between the middle of the letter "a" and the end of the letter "b." There is therefore a certain degree of superimposition within the letter "a" between the two subvariants of the P.38 having the "ac40" code. On the other hand, there is no difference concerning markings and stamps applied to the "ac40" standard model, outside of the fact that the small "ac" under the barrel is no longer present.

The finish on these P.38s machined in 1940 is of a very high quality, showing a superb polished bluing. The black, striated grips in Bakelite, which were standard from this point on, were also numbered. The end of the year 1940, which had seen more than four successive different codes, witnessed an acceleration in the production of the P.38. But very few of them took part in the fighting during the campaigns of Belgium and France. The very high degree of finish on these pistols, as well as the "duality" of the figure "40," justifiably makes them weapons that are actively sought by collectors.

CODE "AC41"

In 1941, the production of the P.38 was estimated at 110,000. Walther, still the only manufacturer, entered a phase of mass production. There were three

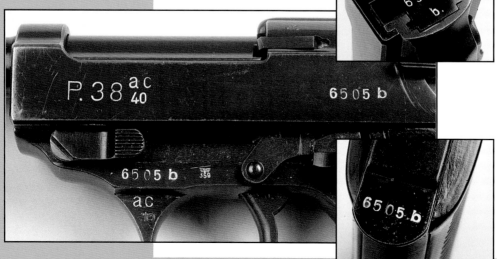

subvariants of the P.38 "ac41," which were based on the finish and the markings:

1. The first subvariant was characterized by a beautiful shiny finish identical to that on the previous models, as well as by the marking "ac" on the left side of the frame, level with the forward part of the trigger guard. The numbers of this series go from "1" to mid-"b."

2. The second subvariant is identifiable by the removal of the aforementioned "ac," but it kept the high-level finish. The serial numbers go from mid-"b" to mid-"i."

3. The third subvariant lost the small "ac" along with the famous prewar Walther shiny finish. This was replaced by a duller finish known as "military" and would remain until the end of the conflict. Some main parts (such as the barrel) of these final subvariant P.38s sometimes have a "rust" color finish. They are found in the range from mid-"g" to the end of "j."

It should be noted that there is a superimposition between the serial numbers of the second and third subvariants. No change is observed concerning the markings. The ridged grips are in black.

In 1941, it was the external aspect that changed considerably. The P.38 was given the opportunity to prove itself on the many battlefields of Europe and North Africa.

CODE "AC42"

With an average of 10,000 P.38s assembled per month, the total number assembled by Walther in 1942 was 120,000. The German High Command nonetheless realized that Walther alone could not satisfy the huge demand for the P.38 since Nazi Germany was fighting on several fronts, from the steppes

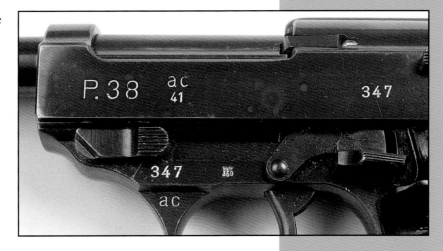

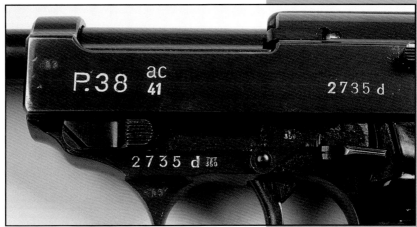

Repeat of the magazine serial number

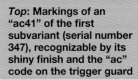

Repeat of the serial number on the base of the barrel

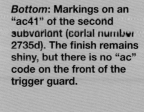

Top: Markings of an "ac41" of the first subvariant (serial number 347), recognizable by its shiny finish and the "ac" code on the trigger guard

Bottom: Markings on an "ac41" of the second subvariant (serial number 2735d). The finish remains shiny, but there is no "ac" code on the front of the trigger guard.

An "ac41" belonging to the third subvariant (serial number 119j). The finish is a military type, and the code ac is not repeated on the trigger guard.

Details of stamps: the military test stamp (eagle/swastika) is surrounded by two military inspection stamps (eagle/359).

1. The first subvariant concerns the P.38 where all the small parts still have the eagle/359 stamp. It seems that this custom disappeared midway through the letter "b" (corresponding to approximately 15,000 examples).

2. The second subvariant is composed of P.38s on which the small parts are no longer tested.

Markings on an "ac42" belonging to the first subvariant (serial number 1811a)

Military inspection stamp (eagle/359) on the left side of the hammer of the "ac42" (serial number 1811a)

of Russia to the Libyan desert. The Zella-Mehlis firm therefore joined up with two other "comanufacturers" (Spreewerke and Mauser) to assist with production.

Concerning more specifically the P.38 bearing the code "ac42," it can be ascertained that the serial numbers range between "1" and the end of the letter "k."

Drawing on the presence of military inspection stamps (the WaffenAmt standard), two subvariants of the "ac42" can be distinguished:

This change in attitude corresponds to the ever-increasing concern of gaining time by removing a series of steps. The conversion from the first to the second subvariant was carried out progressively.

The general finish of these weapons is similar to that which has already been described for the third subvariant of the year 1941. These pistols conserved, however, a remarkably well-finished external appearance. The grips are of a standard type in black Bakelite. There are no modifications in the position of markings in relation to what was described for the end of the year 1941.

The Walther "vintage" year of 1942 has scarcely any structurally significant modifications. Other P.38s dated 42 (for Mauser) or assembled in this same year (for Spreewerke) make their first appearance.

CODE "AC43"

The Walther firm made 150,000 examples in 1943, and this was the year that the firm assembled its highest number of P.38s.

Markings on an "ac42" of the second subvariant (serial number 3923k); it no longer has military inspection stamps on "small parts."

German soldiers on campaign: the man standing on the vehicle has, it would appear, a P.38 holster. *ECPA*

The serial numbers range from "1" to the end of the letter "n." As was the custom at Walther, numbering started at 1 at the beginning of every year.

Two subvariants of "ac43" can be identified. They are based on the morphology and the position of the two code letters and the date:

1. The first subvariant is found in the lineage of the "ac40" codes up to the code "ac42." The "ac43" is positioned just after the P.38 marking and is over two lines ("ac" over "43"). It is generally estimated that it includes numbers from "1" to mid-"1."

2. The second subvariant sees the code-year marking move in relation to the safety lever, and this same code appears on a single line ("ac" followed by "43").

The serial numbers go from mid-"1" to the end of the letter "n."

The finish of these pistols remains more than adequate, bearing in mind the number produced.

The military inspection marks (eagle/359) are localized on the left side of the frame, the right side of the slide (in duplicate), the barrel, and the locking bolt. The military inspection marks (eagle/swastika) are found on the right side of the slide, the barrel, and the locking bolt.

It should be noted that of the many modifications that punctuated the production of the P.38, the shape of the trigger guard was modified in 1943.

The appearance of a small protuberance at the level of the slide stop definitively transforms the shape of the trigger guard, which took on a "heart" rather than an oval shape. This change persisted throughout the years that followed. The extractor was also modified in 1943. It is important to note that during its existence, the P.38 benefited from nine modifications to its slide and fifteen to the frame. A good number of these modifications are not visible to the naked eye and therefore are difficult to appreciate without recourse to technical documents.

The year 1943 represents therefore a period of transition as far as the marking code year is concerned. This new positioning is found on all the P.38s made in Walther workshops in 1944 and 1945.

CODE "AC44"

In comparison to the year 1943, the number of specimens assembled by the Walther firm started to lag; for the year 1944, production is estimated at 130,000. It should be remembered that Walther was involved in the manufacture

Markings on an "ac43" of the first subvariant, bearing the serial number 4099i. The year code is on two lines.

Repeat of the serial number on the base of the barrel

Marking on an "ac43" of the second type of subvariant, bearing the serial number 7818n. The year code was repositioned and is on one line.

Details of stamps: two military inspection stamps (eagle/359) with a military test stamp (eagle/swastika)

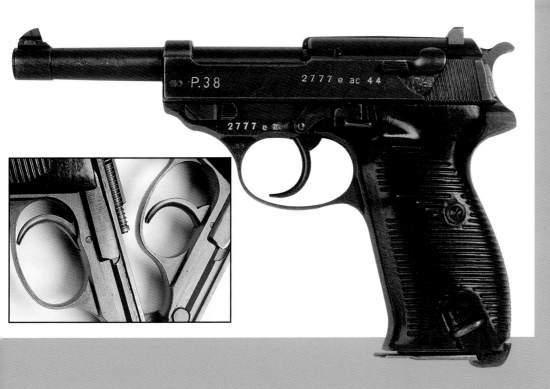

General view of an "ac44" (serial number 2777e), presenting a rust-colored frame and barrel

Comparison of the shape of the trigger guard: *left*, the new trigger guard in the shape of a heart, and *right*, the older, oval-shaped trigger guard

1. Markings on an "ac44" (serial number 2777e), with a frame and barrel with a russet color

2. Military inspection stamp eagle/WaA76 (badly stamped)

3. Code "fnh" applied on a barrel from the Boehmische Waffenfabrik

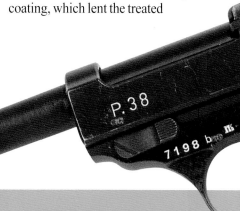

parts a greenish color. The contrast between the two colors is nonetheless a lot less obvious on these partly "rust-colored" "ac44," and consequently they cannot be referred to as "two tone." Some Walther PP (in 7.65 mm caliber) that came out of the workshop at the same time also had this type of finish, although it is important to note that it is an original finish that has nothing to do with any possible rebronzing process.

The ridged grips in brownish Bakelite are of the standard type.

Concerning the markings, the sequence started at the end of 1943 is repeated: the "P.38" followed by the serial number and then the "ac44" code (on the same line) from the extreme left of the slide. The military inspection stamps (eagle/359) are on the right side of the slide, the barrel, and the locking block.

In addition to (or instead of) these standard markings, sometimes others can be found:

1. An eagle/WaA76 stamp, which accompanies the code "fnh" on a certain number of barrels. These were manufactured in Czechoslovakia at the Boehmische Waffenfabrik. They were marked on-site, then sent to Zella-Mehlis. They are principally found on the P.38 "ac44" and "ac45," even though it is not impossible to find a P.38 "ac42" fitted with such a barrel (with the same number).

2. Walther also received frames, slides, and possibly locking blocks from occupied FN (Fabriqué Nationale d'Armes Herstal) in Belgium. Some of these components (aside from the locking bolts) have the eagle/WaA140 stamp.

of numerous other weapons of war (for example, the G43 semiautomatic rifle).

The serial numbers range from "1" to mid-"1." Walther had put the counter back to zero at the beginning of the year.

When examined closely, it is noticeable that the finish deteriorates in a gradual manner, the bronzing is thinner, and the traces of machining are a little more visible. Some P.38s of this period are provided with a frame or barrel that presents a copper aspect (or a rust color), very different from the usual blue. It would appear that for obvious reasons of productivity, the concentration of bluing salts was modified during the last months of the war. Another parameter that must be considered in this technical context is the modification of the contact time between the unpolished metal and the baths containing the bluing salts. The ultimate objective of all these strategies was clearly to reduce the manufacture time and reduce production costs. A parallel is established with a series of P.38s made by the Mauser company starting at the end of 1944. A certain number of these had a dual-color finish that brought together the standard bluing technique with that of phosphate coating, which lent the treated

WaA140

Military Inspection Stamp eagle/WaA140. DWM Werk Lüttich

General view of an "ac45" (serial number 7198b) with "small parts" having a phosphatized finish

Detail of the markings: there is only a single military inspection stamp (eagle/359) with a military test mark (eagle/swastika).

These P.38s marked "ac44" are not especially rare and are still frequently seen in dealers and in private collections. They constitute "standard types" that were part of the mass production carried out in a context of ever-growing shortages in raw materials.

CODE "AC45"

During the first four months of 1945, it is estimated that the Zella-Mehlis firm assembled on the order of 32,000 P.38s. They had the code "ac45."

Generally speaking, the P.38 "ac45" can be divided into two categories:

1. The first concerns weapons on which all the serial numbers corresponded; in other words, the same number found in the usual locations. This first subvariant goes from 1 to 2000c.

2. The second, from 2000c to the letter "d," corresponded to those P.38s on which the serial numbers did not match.

The difficult work conditions that existed at the beginning of 1945, together with an increasingly pressing demand for weapons of all types, could explain the low importance

attributed to the numbering of the P.38. A rapprochement deserves to be made with some Walther PP (code "ac," in 7.65 mm caliber) assembled in '45, which also have numbers that do not correspond.

Predictably, the general finish of the P.38 "ac45" turned slightly worse over time. Walther applied a more perfunctory bluing at that period, which they associated with certain phosphatized "small parts." Some of these "small parts" were not treated at all and as such have kept the natural-metal color. On the other hand, main parts with a "rust"-colored finish (frame, barrel, and slide) are also found, as has been described for the P.38 "ac44." Walther never applied the phosphatizing technique on the main components of the P.38.

There is also a modification in the shape of the (external) hammer. The ten or so small grooves that serve to arm the hammer are replaced by three wider and deeper slide grips. This change was meant to improve the grip of the hammer by the thumb. Walther does not have the exclusivity of this modified hammer, since it is also found on P.38s assembled by Spreewerke at the end of the conflict.

The grips on the "ac45" well illustrate the serious lack of raw materials that all German industry suffered from, and as a result their appearance could differ greatly. Occasionally the internal side of the grips of the "ac45" bore the name of the manufacturer: Durofoe in a diamond shape.

Concerning the markings, the sequence of the sign P.38 is at the front of the slide (left side), followed by the serial number and, last, the "ac" code (still on one line). The stamp appears much less deep, and the alignment of the characters leaves a lot to be desired. The standard proof stamps (military test stamps and military inspection stamps) are also situated in the usual places. It is noted however that the right side of the slide has only a single eagle/359 stamp. It seems that Walther alone made "savings" concerning this stamp in 1945.

Small phosphatized parts

Comparison of hammers: *top*, the new type with wider slide grips, and *below*, the old type with narrower ones

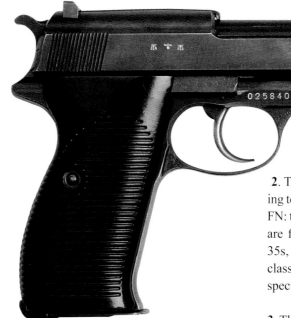

1. A series of pistols (between the numbers 2572 A and 7874 A) presenting a capital letter *A* as a suffix on the frame.

2. The presence of other markings bringing to mind a probable connection with the FN: the letters *MI* or *M* on the frame, which are found on some FN Browning model 35s, which became P640(b) in German classification. The enigmatic figure "35," specific to Walther, is seen occasionally.

3. The more frequent presence of a mysterious asterisk, the meaning of which is disputed. It represents a sort of eight-pointed star.

MI marking, illustrating a highly likely connection with Liege

In addition, following on from what has already been mentioned on the subject of the code "ac44," some P.38 "ac45" examples with Czech barrels, coming directly from Boehmische Waffenfabrik, are often seen. They are marked with the code "fnh" and have the eagle/WaA76 stamp. Rarer are the "ac45" equipped with frames (or slides), which come from the FN (Belgium). To recognize them, look carefully with a magnifying glass at the WaffenAmt stamps: the presence of an eagle/WaA140 stamp indicates an origin in the FN factory in Liege.

But the P.38 "ac45" is still likely to have other particularities, including the following:

4. A certain number of variants (more or less unique) concerning these late assemblies that are pointed out by collectors from time to time. This concerns weapons that have been directly seized (at different stages of manufacture) in the workshop chains of production by liberating forces. Consequently, their degree of finish as well as their markings can vary greatly. All of them give the impression of being "unfinished."

In April 1945, it was American troops that first went into the Walther factories. The GIs helped themselves to a large quantity of handguns. These "late" P.38s were not used on the battlefield, and as a result these weapons are in excellent condition more than seventy years after their conception.

THE HP MODEL

The HP (Heeres Pistole) corresponds to the commercial version of the P.38. Its production was continued on a small scale throughout World War II.

A certain number of these HP weapons were acquired (and tested) by the German military authorities. The total production of these military HPs is estimated at 6,200.

There are three variants that can be differentiated by their finish and markings:

The characteristic position of the serial number on the slide: 025840 (the zero is hidden by the barrel of the weapon)

1. First variant. This has the glossy finish of the HP and P.38 of the period prior to the end of 1941. They have a complete Walther company logo* on the left side of the slide, commercial stamps of the eagle/N type, and the military inspection stamp (eagle/359) on the right side of the slide. The serial number is stamped on the right side of the frame, level with the front of the trigger guard and the base of the barrel.

The slide must be moved back to reveal the serial number, which is on the forward part of the slide. Production is estimated at 2,400 specimens, and the serial numbers are from 11332 to 15705.

2. Second variant. It has a typically military finish, identical to that applied by Walther from the end of 1941 onward. A certain number of specimens machined at that period have the particularity of a distinctly red-colored frame. There are also alterations to the finish resulting from the bluing process, following the modifications of concentration of the chemical products and temperature.

The applied markings are identical to those described for the first variant. Its production is estimated to be 2,600. Last, it should be noted that significant superpositions on the serial numbers between the three different variants took place. The range for the second variant is from 17028 to 23734.

3. Third variant. It is still called code "ac zero" series. It no longer has the logo and the inferior military-type finish, which inevitably deteriorate. The Walther logo is replaced by the date code "ac45" placed just next to the safety lever.

The serial number does not change position (right side of the frame, forward of the trigger guard) but has a zero added. This zero could signify a nonstandard military manufacture. Concerning the acceptance stamps, the commercial marking (eagle/N) disappeared and two military inspection stamps (eagle/359) appear on the right side of the slide, surrounding the military test stamp (eagle/swastika).

This small production is estimated at only 1,200. This numbering ranges approximately from 025900 to 027700.

With this third variant of the HP military model, assembled in the last months of the Third Reich, we arrive at the end of the development of the military P.38.

The superb HP model represents the pistol that tipped the scales in favor of the P.38 at the time when the German military authorities were looking for a replacement for the P.08.

It was this same HP model, "remilitarized" with the means available and provided with a minimalist finish, that was to take part in the last combats of the battle of Berlin.

* The logo applied by Walther on the left side of the slide was as follows: Waffenfabrik Walther, Zella-Mehlis (Thür) Mod HP Walther's Patent Cal. 9m/m.

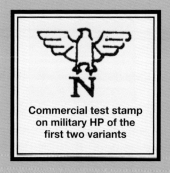

Commercial test stamp on military HP of the first two variants

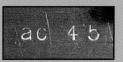

Comparison of late-war markings on a P.38 and an HP model

CHAPTER 3

SPREEWERKE

Entente Cordiale between American and Soviet combatants: the GI in the foreground has a P.38 in his right hand, while his Russian friend has a P.08.

General view of a standard P.38 coming from the Spreewerke factory workshops (serial number 1842 I)

Details of stamps: two military control stamps (eagle/88) surrounding a military test stamp (eagle/swastika)

Details of the markings present on the left side of the P.38 bearing the number 1842 I

The P.38s produced by the Spreewerke factories (Spreewerke GmbH, Metall-warenfabrik, Berlin-Spandau, located in the suburbs of Berlin) have long been neglected, even "snubbed," by collectors. Apart from the aforementioned site in Berlin, this production also concerned a subdivision of the factory situated in the town of Hadrek and Nisu in Czechoslovakia.

It is indisputable that Spreewerke did not have the reputation of manufacturers such as Mauser or Walther. However, Spreewerke, which entered the competition as the second contracting party (i.e., ahead of Mauser), assembled no fewer than 285,000 P.38s between mid-1942 and April 1945.

For the amateur collector, these P.38s are of an undeniable interest due to a series of particularities that set them apart.

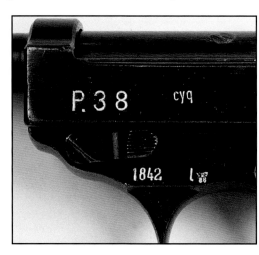

CODE "CYQ"

These P.38s are easily identifiable by their three-letter code: "cyq" (and also "cvq"). Another particularity is the fact that the date of manufacture does not appear at any time, and in this way Spreewerke differentiates itself from the other two manufacturers. The military inspection stamps applied by the inspectors are also very different: the eagle/88 stamp seen in the usual areas—that is, the barrel, frame, slide (two eagles/88, on the right side), and locking bolt. The military test stamps (eagle/swastika) are found on the right side of the slide, the barrel, and the locking bolt. It should nonetheless be pointed out that the very first specimens produced (approximately from 1 to 500) present an eagle/359-type stamp on all small parts (trigger, hammer, slide cover), illustrating a close collaboration between Spreewerke and Walther.

Specialized literature on the subject relates the existence of two "ultra early" types, with an eagle/211-type stamp on the trigger.

MARKINGS

The system of numbering of the P.38s from Spreewerke workshops was also different from that used by Walther and, to a lesser extent, by Mauser. Spreewerke started, quite simply, by applying the numbers 1 up to 9999, thereby constituting a first group (without a letter). Next, a letter "a" was added as a suffix on the following 1,000 weapons (number 1a up to 9999a, making up group "a") and so on. This long series was finished two years and several months later with the number 9999z. This means in essence that the "counters" were not put back to zero at the beginning of 1943 and 1944. The small letter is found as a suffix and changes, in alphabetical order, with each group of 10,000 specimens. The P.38s (called "standard") marked "cyq" are the most frequently encountered in arms fairs and collections. This series, which includes 270,000 weapons, seems to come to an end around January 1945. At that date the small letter came back into service, but in another position: as a prefix. After a first group of 10,000 with a prefix "a," it was then the turn of the letter "b" and then the letter "c," about which doubts remain as to its real purpose. Several P.38 examples bearing the prefix "c" were localized in the United States during the 1960s and 1970s. Their low serial numbers tend to prove that they represent the end of production. In addition, it should be noted that the P.38 series with the "a" and "b" prefixes are associated with the code "cvq."

At that period, Spreewerke also began a series called zero ("cyq" zero series), so called since the serial number of the weapon was preceded by the figure 0. This series could correspond to a nonstandard production. The finish of these P.38s is one of the most rudimentary that has ever existed. These pistols show very many traces of machining, and their external aspect confirms the lack of care concerning the bronzing. They are also characterized by the very unusual presence of another type of military inspection stamp: namely, the eagle/88 stamp replaced by the letter "U" (in capitals, but of a reduced size; "U" meaning *Untersuchung*, i.e., "tested"). It is found on the frame (left side) of the barrel

and the slide (right side) and the barrel. These pistols present in addition the particularity of either the code "cvq," or "ac43" or "ac44" (on two lines). These "ac" codes illustrate their part origin in the FN factory in Liege. The total production of the zero series "cyq" is estimated at fewer than 10,000 specimens (possibly 4,000 to 6,000 at the most). The majority of the indexed serial numbers are between 010 and 05600. The several specimens remaining are found in the 09000 range of numbers. There is consequently a hole in production, for which several explanations have been put forward. It is cited, for example, that entire batches of these P.38s disappeared at the end of the war during bombing raids, or these same batches were dispersed on the occasion of their sale in Europe and the United States after the war. Others mention, perhaps more pragmatically, errors in transcribing the serial numbers in the data bank, or, quite simply, fakes.

To complicate things even more, there exists a series of P.38s called "cyq" double-zero series. As its name indicates, this comes from the fact that the serial number of these pistols is preceded by two zeros. Only a small number of these P.38s have been indexed to date. A certain number (if not the totality) of those came back from the Ukraine, or, unfortunately for the purist, they were rebronzed in the years following the end of the Second World War. Specialists estimate this production at fewer than 100. It seems that the known serial numbers range from 008 to 00100. These pistols bear the code "cvq" on the left side of the slide,

Detail of the markings of a P.38 belonging to the "cyq" zero series (serial number 02204). The letter "U" is easily visible on the frame and the barrel rail.

Markings of a P.38 part of the "cyq" prefix "a" series. In fact, the manufacturers code looks more like a "cvq."

Details of the stamps applied on the right side of the slide on a P.38 belonging to the "cyq" zero series

General view of a P.38 of the "cyq" zero series (serial number 02204)

This soldier of the Wehrmacht, preparing to lift an MG34, has a P.38 holster on his left hip along with two stick grenades. *ECPA*

Opposite page: An early P.38 from the Spreewerke workshops (code "cyq," serial number 8699) placed on the rear side of a first-type holster (personalized by its owner), with a partly loaded spare magazine (code "jvd"), a cloth eagle of the Luftwaffe, an insignia of the Flak (Heeres Flakabziechen), a small leaflet on the recognition of aircraft, and a box of sixteen DWM 7.65 mm cartridges

as well as the military inspection stamps identical to those described for the "single" zero series (type "U" markings rather than the eagle/88).

FINISH

The bad finish on the P.38s from the Spreewerke workshops has, over time, become almost legendary. Only the first 30,000 specimens benefited from an adequate degree of finish, even though it is a far cry from the glossy polish on an HP or a Walther of the pre-1941 period.

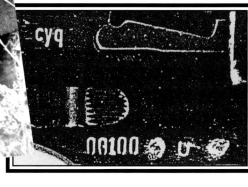

Markings of a "cyq" double-zero series

Comparison of the finish between an early make of P.38 "cyq" (no letter after the serial number) and a later example with the letter "y" as a suffix

Following on from this, the finish progressively altered; traces and machining marks were more and more visible, and the matte bronzing became more perfunctory; the priority seemed to be quantity rather than high quality. It should be noted, however, that unlike Mauser and Walther, it would appear that Spreewerke did not use the phosphatizing technique on their P.38s. Some exceptions were identified, however. It is easy to observe when examining the markings that the alignment of the characters is far from being perfect and that the stamp is not very deep.

The Bakelite grips on the Spreewerke P.38s are as a general rule a "chocolate" color, as distinct from the brownish and black grips on Mauser or Walther P-38s. The manufacturer's logo is found on the inner side.

Following instructions and directives from Walther, the shape of the trigger guard was modified during 1943. It should be remembered that numerous modifications were periodically carried out throughout the period of production and that many of them are not visible to the naked eye.

A view of the "cyq" (serial number 966t) with an asterisk at the level of the left side of the barrel rail and another on the frame

Asterisk applied on the right side of the barrel rail and left side of the frame

Illustrations of markings applied on the frame of the P.38 machined by Spreewerke. The left grip must be removed to render them visible.

At the end of 1944 (or beginning of 1945), a modification appeared, arising from the level of the small surface for the arming of the hammer. It is identical to the one mentioned for the P.38 "ac45."

The relatively bad finish of these weapons does not appear to have affected their functioning.

FEATURES

The other characteristics found at Spreewerke include the following: A supplementary number on the right side of the barrel rail; the significance of these numbers (or codes?), which seem to go in increasing order as production advanced, is unknown. The letter "B" (in capitals) is found fairly systematically, followed by a small figure or a letter. A small "cyq" stamp is frequently stamped on the left side of the barrel rail; it is made visible by pulling the slide back.

In the same manner, when the left pistol grip is dismantled, another series of stamped figures become visible, also with an unknown significance. These numbers are on the frame, hidden by the upper left part of the grip.

The asterisk tends to be found much more frequently on P.38s from Spreewerke factories; a (contested) theory states that this "daisy" corresponds to the result of a strength test. But this hypothesis is far from having unanimous support.

Spreewerke received a small quantity of machined and tested frames (eagle/WaA140 stamp present on the block x) in Liege (Werk

on the barrel. The letters "cyq" are found, even on the P.38 "cvq," in a smaller size stamped on the left side of these barrels. Finally, even if these code modifications were foreseen at the end of 1944, it must be pointed out that Walther, for example, used the same code, "ac," until the end of the war.

On the other side of the debate, some think that this change is intentional, stressing the fact that similarities between the codes are not exceptional, and citing the example of the codes "dot," "dov," and "dou," all of which had been allocated to different subdivisions of the same company (the Waffenwerke Brunn A-G). It is known that the code of a manufacturer that had ceased operations (as was the case for the Waggonfabrik Joseph Rathgeber A-G) could later be allocated to another factory. This tactic helped increase the sought-after confusion. For supporters of this theory, the fact that the barrels of these P.38s marked "cvq" have a marking "cyq" is

Lüttich), as well as slides marked "ac43" and "ac44" (year code on two lines). These last ones are in fact included in the "cyq" zero series.

A certain number of abnormalities regarding markings and other acceptance stamps have been reported more frequently on the P.38. These include "cyq" printed backward, a supplementary eagle/88 stamp on the right side of the slide, and a back-to-front letter "c" (suffix).

CODE "CVQ" CONTROVERSY

This possible change of code is incredibly controversial, given the similarity between the two codes: "cyq" and "cvq" differ by only a single letter in the same position.

On one side there are supporters of the theory who say that the code "cvq" is just an accident: the stamp of the "y" lost its lower part and therefore became a "v." It is true that in a system of random allocation of new codes, it is highly unlikely that Spreewerke was attributed a code so close to the previous one. In addition, it is known that at the beginning of the conflict, the code "cvq" was allocated to another factory (Waggonfabrik Joseph Rathgeber A-G, Munich), which appears to have been an industrial partner of Spreewerke. It is clear that the "cvq" code never appeared

Other markings of unknown meaning: supplementary numbering on the right side of the barrel rails

This army noncommissioned officer (NCO) has on his left side a first-model holster for a P.38. The extension of the belt buckle gives the impression that this holster has been modified. *ECPA*

Comparison of the codes "cyq" and "cvq"

This Heer motorcyclist wears his P.38 in its holster on a belt.

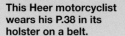

not an argument valid enough to exclude any deliberate change of code. It is highly likely that, since the production of barrels was sufficiently advanced compared to that of the slides, the Germans did not have enough time to apply the new code on the barrels. This gap in production and marking on the different components is not exceptional. In these circumstances, a period of transition during which several markings coexisted must be considered. In addition, it is surprising that for some years, Spreewerke assembled tens of thousands of P.38s with no mention of a faulty letter. Last, it seems that the shape of the letters of the "cvq" code remains very similar throughout its existence. This code remains constant in its appearance, and if irregularities on the surface and the effects of the finish are taken into consideration, this argument advocates against the existence of a broken letter, which would by definition give a greater disparity in the markings.

Whatever the case, the question will not be decided as long as the supposed official documents do not support one theory over another.

In practice, the "cvq" code concerns the "standard" P.38 from half of the "z" group (or "w," depending on the source), some "a" and "b" prefix series (and possibly "c"?) and some single- and double-zero series. Typically, this pertains essentially to the end of production of the P.38 by the Spreewerke factory.

CONCLUSION

In conclusion, it can be confirmed that Spreewerke fulfilled its contract concerning the manufacture of P.38 pistols more than honorably. It must be borne in mind that this enterprise was fundamentally specialized in the manufacture of barrels, howitzers, and other parts for the artillery. It is remarkable that by way of Spreewerke, the P.38 was to be the only German-designed semiautomatic pistol assembled in a foreign country (occupied Czechoslovakia).

Production was interrupted at the end of April 1945, when Red Army forces occupied Berlin and the surrounding area. Its industrial sites were then dismantled by the Soviets. The Czechs went on to produce a small series of the P.38.

CHAPTER 4

MAUSER

Peter Paul Mauser (1838–1914) and his brother Wilhelm Mauser (1834–1882), from the small town of Oberndorf-am-Neckar in Württemberg, were behind the fantastic development of the Mauser Waffenfabrik.

Creator of the revolutionary bolt-action rifle (with the 1871 model infantry rifle), this famous firm contributed to the development of a great number of (light) weapons that were used throughout the world.

It designed other long weapons, including the 98 model Mauser rifle, the C96 Mauser pistol, antitank rifles in 13 mm caliber, and the 1914 model semiautomatic pistol. Between 1900 and 1930, the DWM, for its part, assembled more than a million military and civilian P.08s. In 1922, the DWM changed its name and became the BKIW (Berlin-Karlsruher Industrie-Werk). During the 1920s, conforming to the restrictions imposed by the Treaty of Versailles, the Mauser company produced industrial sewing machines, precision weighing instruments, and even small automobiles.

At the beginning of the 1930s, the P.08 assembly lines were transferred from BKIW (Berlin) to Mauser (Oberndorf). Apart from the machine tools, this transfer involved an enormous stock of weapons and spare parts. In this context of concealed remilitarization, the Mauser-Werke A-G assembled a series of P.08s from existing parts. These weapons were destined for German military and paramilitary organizations, as well as some foreign markets (Dutch contracts, P.08 Stoeger in the United States).

In 1934, Mauser won the contract for manufacturing the P.08 for the German army.

This large contract did not prevent them from assembling other semiautomatic pistols: the Mauser 1914/34 and 1934 in 7.65 mm caliber, the HSc in 7.65 mm caliber, and the Mauser C96 in 7.63 mm caliber (among others). The Mauser-Werke also contributed to the development of MG34, MG81, and MG151 machine guns; the Flak 38 antiaircraft gun barrel; and the standard 98k model infantry rifle.

In competition to replace the aging P.08, the HSc pistol proposed by the Mauser company was outclassed by the HP Walther model during tests carried out at the end of the thirties. However, it was not before the end of 1942 that Mauser started manufacture of the P.38.

The industrial buildings of the company were little affected by Allied bombing up to mid-1943, but after that date, air raids were much more frequent. On April 20, 1945, the Oberndorf site was occupied by French troops.

CODE "BYF42"

At the end of 1942, it was the turn of Mauser to start the chain of production for the P.38. This production is estimated to stand at 19,000. But it is thought that only 700 P.38s were in fact assembled in 1942, all others being assembled in 1943.

German NCO sporting a superb first-model P.38 holster on his left hip

A P.38 marked "byf42" (serial number 5683), with a P.08 made the same year, a box of sixteen rounds 9 mm Parabellum (type SE), a War Merit Cross, and a General Assault Badge.

Details of the stamps: two
military inspection stamps
(eagle/135) surrounding
a military test stamp
(eagle/swastika)

*Opposite page: From top
to bottom*, the Mauser
Schnellfeuer pistol (or 712
model) fitted with its
twenty-round magazine, a
P.38 with the "byf42" code
(serial number 5a), and a
Mauser 1934 pistol of the
Kriegsmarine. Each of
these is accompanied by a
box of twenty rounds (two
magazines of ten), a
7.63 mm Mauser of the
DWM, a box of sixteen
9 mm Parabellum
cartridges (code "aux,"
year 1942), and a box of
twenty-five lacquered
7.65 mm rounds of
the DWM.

Markings present on the
left side of the "byf42"
serial number 5683

Markings present on the
left side of the "byf42"
serial number 5a

The serial numbers ranged, in theory, from between number "1" and the end of the letter "a," but it seems that some specimens bear the letter "c." Basing the argument on the presence or absence of military inspection stamps on certain parts, it is possible to distinguish two subvariants of the P.38 "byf42" code:

1. The first subvariant concerns the "byf42" with the small parts (hammer, trigger, slide stop, locking bolt, and so on) that have an eagle/135. These specimens are extremely rare since it is reckoned that only the first 800 to 1,000 "byf42" seem to have benefited from these WaffenAmt "extras."

2. The second subvariant comprises all the other "byf42." The small parts were no longer tested. In comparison it should be remembered that Walther abandoned this practice in early 1942, and Spreewerke never used it.

The finish of these first P.38s from the workshops of the Oberndorf firm was very distinctive. The bluing on the slides has a relatively pale-blue to black tint. This matte finish is unique and a feature of the first P.38s assembled by Mauser. It must not be confused with a possible rebronzing. Despite this feature, these P.38s remain very well made. The Bakelite grips with longish ridges are of a standard type.

The markings applied on these weapons are also of a standard type. On the left side of the slide, going from the front to the rear, are the initials "P.38" followed by the Mauser code "byf" on the figure "42," and, last, the serial number. This is stamped in a slightly higher position in relation to its counterpart at Walther. The minuscule letter that accompanies the serial number above the first 10,000 specimens is applied in italics (at least on the first 260,000 parts). The serial number is repeated on the left side of the frame, the barrel, and the locking bolt. The military inspection stamps are distributed on the pistol in the usual way. The eagle/135 stamp is therefore found on the left side of the frame, the barrel, the locking bolt, and in duplicate on the right side of the slide. This also has a military inspection stamp (eagle/swastika). The other two eagle/swastika are on the barrel and the locking bolt.

The features of its bluing, along with its "early make" appearance, make these "byf42"-marked P.38s highly desired among collectors.

CODE "BYF43"

Still involved in the assembly of weapons of war such as the Mauser HSc pistol in 7.65 mm caliber and the 98k rifle with a 20 mm barrel, the firm of Oberndorf-am-Neckar also produced around 162,000 P.38s in 1943, a year representing a real turning point in the Second World War, and the period during which the greatest number of P.38s were assembled.

Mauser HSc military pistol (presence of an eagle/135 on the trigger guard) placed on its leather holster and shown with a box of twenty-five rounds of 7.65 mm caliber

Details of the stamps: two military inspection stamps (eagle/135) surrounding a military test stamp (eagle/swastika)

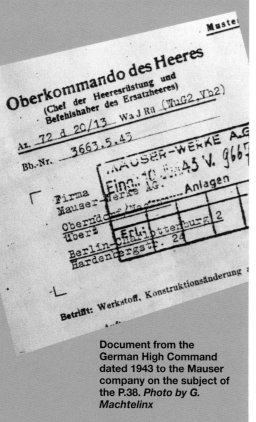

Document from the German High Command dated 1943 to the Mauser company on the subject of the P.38. *Photo by G. Machtelinx*

Markings present on the left side of a "byf43" of the series 8483f

The group including these "byf43" goes from the series without a letter up to the end of the letter "q." A small number of these "byf43" have been indexed in blocks of letters further down the alphabet, in group "r" or even "s." It should be borne in mind the fact that Mauser did not "go back to zero" at the beginning of every year, but there are many zones of superposition in the numbering.

Some authors distinguish, somewhat artificially, two subvariants of the "byf43," depending on the presence of eagle/135- or eagle/WaA135-type military inspection stamps. The first goes from the letter "a" to the end of the letter "p," whereas the second pertains only to the end of the letter "p" and the beginning of the letter "q" (even more so the "strays" from groups "r" and "s"). These P.38s of group "q" sometimes accumulate both types of inspection stamps and consequently were referred to as transitional.

Considering the very high number of P.38s assembled in 1943 the finish on these pistols is very good. Quite logically, the first "byf43" still benefited from the particular finish as has been described for the "byf42." It was during this year that Mauser covered the P.38 with a more standard military bluing. The grips in Bakelite are brown, with reddish hints. Like Walther and Spreewerke, Mauser also applied a series of structural modifications to different components of the pistol. The most visible among them was the change in the shape of the trigger guard by the addition of a small protuberance at the level of the slide stop.

The markings are standard; the sequence (on the left side of the slide) of the initials "P.38," followed by the code "byf" on the figure "43," followed by the serial number. This is repeated to a lesser degree on the frame, the base of the barrel, and the locking bolt (last three figures and the letter).

At Mauser, therefore, there are no modifications of the position and the shape of the year code (as Walther had carried out in 1943). Concerning the military test marks (eagle/swastika), they are easily localized on the right side of the slide and the barrel and on the locking bolt. As for the military inspection stamps, they are found on the left side of the frame (next to the serial number), in duplicate on the right side of the slide, on the barrel, and on the locking bolt. The only development is in relation

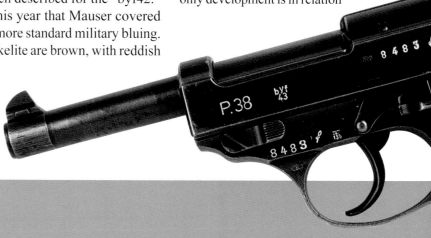

to the transition from the eagle/135 stamp to the eagle WaA135 stamp at the end of 1943.

These P.38s bearing the code "byf43" are not considered as real rarities.

They are, above all, perfect illustrations of military production during wartime.

CODE "BYF44"

The number of P.38s made by the Oberndorf firm in 1944 was as high as 150,000.

The serial numbers are situated between the beginning of the letter "q" and half of the letter "e." The very first "byf44" are nevertheless indexed in the letter "p." Mauser followed the numbering of its P.38s by disregarding the change of year. By acting in this way, the end of the alphabet was reached around autumn 1944. At that date, the firm quite simply started the alphabet again (after the customary series without a letter) to reach the letter "e" at the end of December 1944. It is understandable that there are no two "byf44" bearing the same number. In order to differentiate them even more easily, they are referred to as "byf44" on the first series for the P.38s, ending the alphabet that had started two years earlier, and the second series for the others.

The P.38s "byf44" are also categorized in several subvariants on the basis of the finish and to a lesser extent the markings:

1. The first subvariant concerns the P.38 with a blued finish, which can be described as standard production. Some authors divide this subvariant itself into two, depending on the fleeting presence of type eagle/135 stamps (letter "p" and beginning of the letter "q") or eagle/WaA135-type stamps (all the following).

2. The second subvariant includes the P.38 that was either partly or totally phosphatized.

3. The third subvariant involves some P.38s with the year code "ac43" and "ac44" (on two lines) and eagle/WaA135-type military inspection stamps. The slides are originally of the DWM Werk Lüttich (Belgium). They are detailed in chapter 5, dedicated to the FN during the occupation.

The finish of these "byf44" pistols was initially military bronzing, described for the production of the previous year. The quality of the bronzing diminishes very progressively. During the year 1944, Mauser developed the concept of a phosphatized finish designed to replace the standard bronzing. This finish lent a typically greenish-gray color to metallic parts. This new protective coating was to be applied first on slides and frames; the barrels stayed bronzed. The contrast between the colors is such that the "byf44" is referred to as two tone.

Subsequently, it was the entire weapon that benefited from this particular treatment. The grips made in Bakelite are of a reddish-brown color on the bronzed models and black on the phosphate-treated specimens.

The markings were not subject to any modification. The initial P.38s are found on the left side of the slide, followed by the year code "byf44" (on two lines) and, finally, the serial number. Apart from the slide, this number is repeated on the usual places; in other words, on the left side of the frame, on the barrel, and partially on the locking bolt. The military inspection stamps (eagle/135, then eagle/WaA135) were distributed on the

The army soldier at right holds a P.38 in his right hand and field glasses in his left. Other items can also be identified, such as an MG34, a 98k rifle, and ammunition supplies. *ECPA*

Markings present on the left side of a blued "byf44" (standard production), serial number 6493v

Details of the stamps: two military inspection stamps (eagle/WaA135) surrounding a military test stamp (eagle/swastika)

Fierce fighting during the capture of Kharkov in March 1943

It is also reported that the finish on some of these pistols can be incomplete (parts are unbronzed). In all likelihood, these P.38s were assembled at the very end of the war from a series of spare parts from various sources. It should be noted that one feature of this period is the heterogeneous nature of the assembled weapons. It is highly likely that not all these assemblies have yet been indexed, and it is probable that they never will be. In reality, the collector is occasionally confronted by other types of reassemblies that have the fact that they were made after the end of hostilities as their main characteristic. It is known that a certain number of pistols (and various other accessories) were specially assembled for (and by) GIs. This concerns reassemblies dating from the period immediately after the war.

But these are, of course, more-recent reassemblies that constitute veritable imitations when they are presented as "original" assemblies.

It is principally the change in the finish at the end of 1944 that is of most interest to collectors. Mauser did not have exclusivity on the technique of phosphate coating that the German armaments industry was to apply to a considerable number of small arms of this period (Cz27 and Cz38 semiautomatic pistols, and Sturmgewehr assault rifles). Nonetheless, the two-tone P.38s that came out of Mauser at that time show splendid applications of this technique.

Opposite page: A series of objects surrounding a Mauser-made two-tone P.38 (code "svw45," serial number 2546e) captured by an Allied soldier in Germany, consisting of a reserve magazine with phosphate finish, an SA service dagger, a second type of pebbled leather holster, and a brown Volkstrum armband along with different insignia taken from German uniforms and equipment (a cloth eagle, a Wound Badge, and a cap eagle)

right side of the slide (in duplicate), the left side of the frame, the barrel, and the locking bolt. The same can be said for the military test marks (eagle/swastika), which are present on the right side of the slide, the barrel, and the locking bolt.

One particularity is the existence of a small number of P.38s coded "byf44" with a frame marked "ac" (on the front part, left side of the trigger guard). This "ac" is the same shape as on the P.38 "ac41" of the first subvariant. These pistols are occasionally without any serial numbers. Concerning the military inspection stamps, the eagle/359 type stands alongside the eagle/WaA135 type. The military test marks (eagle/swastika) are usually present.

Right side of a "byf44" with two-tone finish

Markings present on the left side of a "byf44" with a two-color finish, bearing the serial number 7958b

P.38 "byf44" with a blued finish with a CZ 27 pistol with phosphate finish, its holster in brown leather, a box of twenty-five 7.65 mm rounds, and a medal from the Russian front

This British soldier is keeping a very close eye on German prisoners.

CODE "SVW45"

At the beginning of 1945, the Mauser firm was given another code: "svw," going above the figure "45."

The number of P.38s assembled by Mauser under this new code is estimated at 15,000. The P.38 is not unique in having this code, since it is also found on Mauser 98k rifles from the Oberndorf workshops at the beginning of 1945.

Concerning the numbering of the "svw45," it is generally thought that the serial numbers range from the letter "c" to the letter "f." But other authors think that the first "svw45" are situated in groups of earlier letters, thereby overlapping with the end of production of the "byf44." One of the pastimes of some (determined) P.38 collectors consists of "tracking" one of the last (and, if possible, the very last) P.38s assembled by Mauser, before control of the factory was taken over by French troops.

It is believed that production of the Nazi "svw45" finished on April 20, 1945, and that it was taken up again by the French starting on May 10 of that year. The last Nazi "svw45" indexed in a vast database has the serial number 3549f. The first French "svw45" have been identified in a range near the number 8700 g. This theory necessarily implies a continuity between the numbers of German-produced weapons and those used by the French, which is not proven.

Three types of finish have been noted, which have been divided into three subvariants:

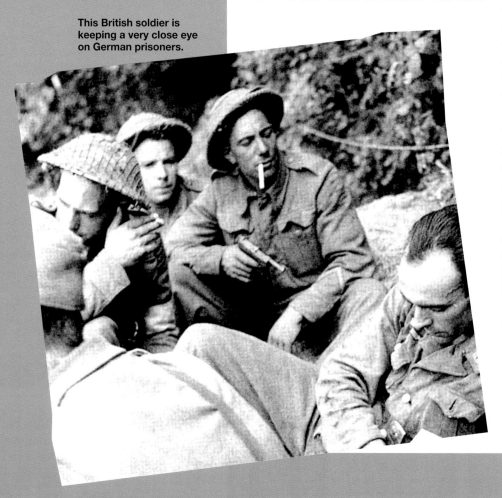

1. The two-tone finish: identical to that described for the P.38 "byf 44"; in other words, a blued barrel with a phosphate-coated frame and slide (along with other smaller parts)

2. The 100% phosphate-coated finish: in this case, the process of phosphate coating was also on the barrel. The weapon took on a uniformly greenish finish.

3. The 100% blued finish, with an absence of any phosphatizing. The reason for this finish is not known. The applied bronzing has revealed itself to be extremely thin and perfunctory. This P.38, with a "svw 45" code and not phosphated, is the most difficult to find, since only a very small number of them were produced.

This famous phosphatizing can take on varying intensities and therefore give an appearance that ranges from gray to green.

The ridged grips are in black Bakelite. Apparently, the Germans did not use metallic (ridged) grips on the "svw45." These remain the prerogative of the "svw45" (and others) assembled by the French.

Concerning the markings, the sequence that has been described previously is found. the left side of the slide has the initials "P.38," then the code "svw45" ("svw45" above "45"), and finally the serial number. This is also found on the same places as previously mentioned many times: the left side of the frame, the barrel, and the locking bolt. Unlike the last P.38s machined by Walther (the "ac45"), it would appear that there are no Nazi "svw45" with serial numbers that are not consistent. The military inspection stamps as well as the military test stamps applied on these pistols are identical to those that have been described for the "byf44"; an eagle/WaA135 on the left side of the frame, the right side of the slide (always in duplicate, unlike the "ac45") surrounding the eagle/swastika, on the barrel, and on the locking bolt. The last two elements also have the eagle/swastika.

Common sense would suggest that the "svw" code would disappear with the Allied victory. However, since French troops occupying the Oberndorf site took up production of the P.38, this did not happen. These pistols are easily recognizable by their uniformly phosphatized appearance, which was the origin of the nickname "Gray Ghost" in American documentation. They are also recognizable by their ridged metallic grips, the "svw 45" code (then "svw 46"), and the small, five-pointed star present on the right side of the slide.

Detail of the stamps: the military test stamp (eagle/swastika) is surrounded by two military inspection stamps (eagle/WaA135).

John Moses Browning

Pictured next to a two-tone P.38 machined in part at the occupied Fabriqué Nationale and a box of cartridges with the code "ch": *Top left*, a pre-1940 FN Browning 1935 model (9 mm Parabellum) with its instruction manual. *Top right*, a 1903 Browning model in 9 mm Long caliber. *Bottom left*, an FN Browning 1900 model in 7.65 mm caliber with a box of rounds of the FN. *Bottom middle*, an FN Browning 1906 model in 6.35 mm caliber.

INTRODUCTION

The association between the brilliant American inventor John Moses Browning and the European partner Fabriqué Nationale d'Armes de Guerre de Herstal (National War Weapons Factory) in Belgium during the year 1898 proved to be very fruitful. A whole host of semiautomatic pistols were made (the FN Browning 1900, 1903, 1906) and had a remarkable and long-lasting international success.

The Germans invaded the kingdom of Belgium, Holland, and the Grand Duchy of Luxembourg at dawn on May 10, 1940. This was the beginning of the Blitzkrieg, which would inflame western Europe throughout the following weeks. The town of Liege fell on May 12, 1940, and the German military authorities went on to seize FN installations starting on May 20, 1940. They transferred weapons and ammunitions found on site to the citadel. German officers spent the following three weeks inspecting these same installations. Belgium capitulated on May 28, 1940. The

FN had to change its name and became the DWM Werk Lüttich. On June 15, 1940, a German officer representing a regional bureau of the WaffenAmt took up office in Brussels.

Production could therefore resume on behalf of the invader. Weapons, weapons components, and ammunition were assembled in the workshops in Liege. A series of senior managers (of DWM and Mauser and others), officers, and other technicians were to succeed one another as head of the factory during the four long years of occupation. This production was described as fairly "chaotic." It should be taken into account that a certain number of important elements would influence this production significantly:

1. The availability of machine tools was far from being optimal. Some of them were sent to Germany, whereas others were "imported" from the Netherlands.

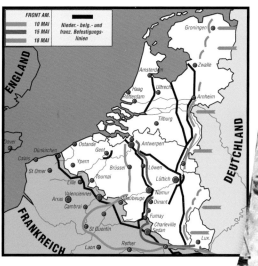

2. The production of P.38 parts was carried out simultaneously with the P640(b) assembly line (among others). **3.** Output (and reliability!) of the workers serving the occupier seems to have been fairly mediocre. The DWM Werk Lüttich had as many as 12,000 workers, particularly at the time of forced labor. The code assigned to the DWM Werk Lüttich was "ch."

At the end of August 1944, the German director received the order to dismantle the factory and bring the machines back to Germany. Considering the military situation, this dismantling operation could only be partial. It should be noted that by the beginning of August 1944, a certain number of these machines had already been sent to Germany. On September 5 6, 1944, the last official German representatives and employees packed up and left, and on September 9 the Sherman tanks of the US 1st Army penetrated the city of Liege. The liberated factory appeared to be in a very bad state. The major part of the machine tools had disappeared, while those remaining were badly damaged, making any kind of precision work difficult, if not impossible. The liberated FN was called on

to contribute to the assembly of tank tracks (400,000) destined for US tanks. In the same vein, a great number of jerry cans were made on site. In spite of everything, the very large number of weapons spare parts found on-site meant, however, that a certain number of handguns (essentially FN 35 model and FN 10/22) could be assembled, ushering in the progressive resumption of activities.

THE P.38 AT LIEGE

There is still some controversy concerning the number of P.38 parts or components that were actually made at Herstal (Belgium) under the control of the occupying forces.

There are two opposing theories, each one based on a very different interpretation of an official report made by two Allied officers (the American major J. H. Crews and the British wing commander A. Day) as a result of their visiting the FN site on November 22–23, 1944.

On one side there are those who consider that a relatively high number of these components destined for the P.38 were manufactured on the Liege site. It emerged from this famous report that 4,720 frames, 2,272 slides, and an unspecified number of locking bolts were found on the assembly lines of the FN. Consequently, from this small number of abandoned parts found on-site, they deduced that the total number of components produced must be very much higher. They calculated that there was a regular delivery throughout a period of about fourteen months (i.e., between June 1943 and August 1944) of these spare parts to the following factories:

Firing training with a P.38 (Russia, May–June 1944)

Detail of the front lines between May 10 and 18, 1940

Representation of a military inspection stamp eagle/WaA140

Details of a military inspection stamp (eagle/ WaA140) on a 1935 FN Browning of the occupation (and a military test stamp, eagle/swastika)

Detail of the markings of the P.38 shown above

Comparison of the "standard" "ac44" marking and "ac43" on two lines

Walther:

Walther would have received about 8,000 P.38 frames that are found on P.38s marked "ac44" and "ac45." These frames were stamped at Liege with the eagle/WaA140 on their left side.

Walther were also supplied with slides that had the same stamp on the right side.

Mauser:

Mauser obtained around 15,000 slides presenting a marking type "ac43" and "ac44," which were not stamped on-site. They have the Oberndorf military inspection stamp; in this case, the eagle/WaA135.

Mauser was not assigned any frames.

Spreewerke:

Spreewerke received a total of around 1,000 parts comprising frames stamped at Liege and slides marked with "ac43" and "ac44."

Partisans of this theory estimate therefore that no fewer than 30,000 frames and slides (along with a large number of locking bolts) were actually manufactured at the DWM Werk Lüttich, and they also claim that it was possible to find the names of three German supervisors who were responsible for the development of this program. This program was still active as of August 1, 1944; in other words, barely five weeks before the German withdrawal. One scarcely has to imagine the scale of the personnel deployed for a "small contract."

In the other camp are supporters (with W. Buxton at the head) of the theory that said that only a small number of P.38 components were machined at DWM Werk Lüttich. This author did not hesitate to question the veracity of the famous aforementioned report. Several arguments are used to support his position:

1. The Allied officers used for this type of mission were not specialists.

2. The report in question did not stipulate if Allied inspectors saw and made an inventory themselves of the frames and slides mentioned.

3. The P.38 components were the only parts of the (German) weapons that were found on-site. There is no mention in this report of other components (for example, destined for the 98k rifle) that were nonetheless manufactured at Liege. It is difficult to imagine the Germans abandoning such precious spare parts. The fact that the P.38 would still be produced for more than seven months from the date of the German withdrawal from Liege should not be overlooked.

4. It is not known what became of these parts that were found on-site. The FN, in these difficult times of reconstruction, could not allow them to be destroyed or even stocked. Such a waste would have been unwarranted in this particularly difficult context. In addition, if these parts had been sold, it is possible that a certain number of pistols assembled in that way would have reappeared at some point. They would have constituted a known variant, in the same way as the "cyq" zero series, for example, yet this was not the case,

Ultimately, for W. Buxton, the manufacture of these components took place over a period of five to six months maximum and corresponded to the prototype stage of development. It was a project that never really took off, and the critical reader will come to his or her own conclusion.

From a practical point of view, there are several principal characteristics of these P.38s at the root of this "partly Belgian" history:

1. Walther received a certain number of slides and frames coming from the FN. The very rare slides are recognizable by the presence of a eagle/WaA140 stamped on the right side alongside a WaA eagle/359 and the eagle/swastika. The letters "ac" stamped on these pistols are very clearly distinct from the letters "ac" usually used by the Walther firm: the larger "ac" of the English-speaking world and a specific typology, which are easily recognizable to a trained eye. In addition, these "ac" letters with their very particular characteristics systematically go above the figures "43" or "44." It can be claimed that any "ac44"

because no such variant has ever come to light either in Europe or the United States. It is only a small step to claim that either these P.38 components never really existed or they existed in very small numbers.

5. Witnesses of this troubled period of history of the FN never mention the presence of significant quantities (i.e., tons) of spare parts destined for the P.38. They also indicate the circulation of very small quantities of this type of material, assigned principally for the repair of weapons in service.

6. The parts coming from the FN appeared in the production of the three contracting parties in 1944, from July to September. They were found sporadically in the months after that period up to 1945. It seems logical to conclude that if the three contracting parties had received the P.38 components during this fourteen-month period, these "hybrid" P.38s would have been seen at Walther, Mauser, and Spreewerke, since very many were assembled during the period in question. However, this was not the case, and in addition it is very difficult to imagine the three previously mentioned contractors storing spare parts during an identical period of time and then using them simultaneously.

7. If there had been more than 7,000 frames and slides, these P.38s would be seen a lot more often on the collectors' market. These P.38s "made in FN" in 1944 are considered as fairly rare, whereas those made in 1945 (and at the Spreewerke) are quite rare.

The army NCO in the foreground wears a first-model P.38 holster (on his left hip). A map holder on the right hip serves as a counterweight. Behind, an MG34 is partly visible.

MI marking illustrating a highly likely connection with Liege

on two lines necessarily constitutes an original piece from Liege. Indeed, the transition from two lines to one took place at the end of 1943. The frames delivered by the FN also have the military inspection stamp (eagle/WaA140) on their left side. Those P.38s subject to these specific markings are the "ac44" in the group "g" and "h," and the "ac45" in the group "c." It must be noted that Walther, the holder of the "ac" code, was assigned only a very small number (estimated at 120) of slides bearing this code. In addition, they were the only slides bearing the military inspection stamp eagle/WaA140.

2. Mauser received only slides marked "ac43" and "ac44" on two lines. These slides were not tested on-site, and consequently no eagle/WaA140-type stamp was detected. The letters "ac" presented on these pistols have the same characteristics as those described earlier for the (rare) slides delivered to the Walther firm. These P.38s from the Oberndorf workshops and having the code "ac" therefore have eagle/WaA135-type military inspection stamps. They are

found in the "c," "d," and "e" groups of letters (in the range of "byf44"). Other specimens are destined for the German police; their serial number has no letter, and they bear a specific eagle/F-type stamp. These P.38s can have a bronzed, two-tone, or completely phosphate finish. For reasons that are not apparent, Mauser was not assigned frames.

3. Spreewerke was granted slides marked "ac43" and "ac44" (still on two lines), the same as Walther and Mauser. The large "ac" letters are found on the left side of the slide, whereas the right side shows eagle/88-type stamps (and never eagle/WaA140) and eagle/swastika. As already suggested for Mauser, there were also Spreewerke-made P.38s with the "ac" code. A certain number of these P.38s marked "ac43" and "ac44" assembled by Spreewerke form an integral part of the "cyq zero" series. They are particularly well represented in the 03500 to 05600 range. Frames with the eagle/WaA140 on their left side have also been recorded.

On the subject of markings, it should be acknowledged that the majority of these P.38s with components coming from the FN had stamps such as "M" or "MI" on their frame or slide. The meaning of these signs is still unknown. These stamps are also found on the FN model 35 pistols made under occupied control (the P64[b] in German classification). These mysterious markings are in a certain way a sign of their Liege origins. There are also other particularities on these pistols: a Czech-origin barrel (code "fnh"), the figure "35" on Walther weapons, and a mysterious asterisk.

Beyond the debate on the importance of the participation of the occupied FN in the machining of parts for the P.38, it should also be noted that there is agreement that there was no complete assembly of the P.38 at Liege, and the harsh reality for the P.38 collector is that no P.38 has the "ch" code.

CHAPTER 6

THE POLICE P.38

THE WEIMAR PERIOD IS CHARACTERIZED BY A DECENTRALIZED AND VERY WEAKENED POLICE FORCE, ONE REASON FOR THIS BEING THE RESTRICTIONS IMPOSED BY THE TREATY OF VERSAILLES. THE POLICE PROVED INEFFECTIVE IN THEIR FIGHT AGAINST EXTREMIST GROUPS ON BOTH THE LEFT AND THE RIGHT.

From 1933 onward, at the instigation of Hermann Göring (minister of the interior) and Heinrich Himmler (*Reichsführer-SS*), the Nazis took control of the different police forces; a strong police force set up for the service of a dictatorial power. The war on the opposition on all sides (political and others) became the norm. The bloody purge that took place on the night of June 30, 1934, known as "the Night of the Long Knives," well illustrates this state of affairs. Ernst Röhm and other high-ranking SA (Sturmabteilung; Nazi Party paramilitary force) leaders were brutally eliminated.

In 1936, Himmler became chief of German police. He finalized the nationalization of the different police forces, which he placed under the control of the SS High Command. He created the ORPO (Ordnungspolizei), which regrouped a series of specific sections such as the rural, river, and municipal police along with the Sipo (Sicherheitspolizei), which included the Kripo

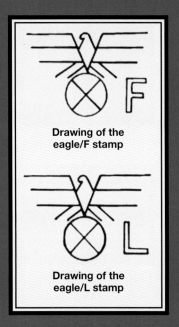

Drawing of the eagle/F stamp

Drawing of the eagle/L stamp

Superimposition of three police markings: *top*, eagle/L of a police Mauser HSc; *middle*, eagle/B on a Sauer & Sohn pistol holster; *bottom*, eagle/C of a police Walther PPK

(criminal police) and the Gestapo (secret police), with its sinister reputation. During the 1939 to 1945 period, the number of these police units grew significantly and their tasks became more varied. Some of them specialized in the fight against the resistance, whereas others were on the front line or carried out administrative work in occupied territories.

PRODUCTION

In a logical fashion, from 1943 onward the P.38 took over from the P.08 within the police forces of the Third Reich. There is no consensus on the exact number of P.38s specifically assigned to the police; production figures vary, depending on the author, from 6,200 to 10,000 examples. Whatever the case, the police P.38 remains a weapon that is considered one of a kind. An overwhelming majority of these pistols came from Mauser company workshops.

As a guideline, the German police were equipped with the following handguns:

- the Walther PPK, in 7.65 mm caliber essentially

- the Walther PP, in 7.65 mm caliber essentially

- the Mauser HSc, in 7.65 mm caliber

- the Mauser Mod. 34, in 7.65 mm caliber

- the Sauer and Sohn Mod. 38, in 7.65 mm caliber

- the Steyr Mod. 1912, in 9 mm caliber

- the P.08, in 9 mm Parabellum caliber

It is immediately clear that it is the 7.65 mm caliber that is the most represented.

MARKINGS

Unlike on the majority of P.38s destined for the other elements of the German armed forces, there are markings specific to the police. They are represented by the letters "K," "F," "L," "C," along with "B" or "D." The P.38 is associated only with the letters "L" and "F." The letters "B" and "D" seem to be reserved for holsters. These "famous" letters accompany a stylized eagle bearing a swastika (or a single X in a circle) in its claws, which is therefore referred to as eagle/L or eagle/F. The precise meaning of these letters is not known and has been the subject of much speculation. It would seem that each letter represents a different material acceptance office for the police, and not a branch or subdivision of this corps. Some speculate, however, on the analogy between the letter "L" and the Landespolizei or the letter "K" with the Komunalpolizei etc. Others, however, have researched geographic links: "K" for Köln (Cologne) or "B" for Berlin. These analogical theories are not convincing, and the thinking, until proven otherwise, is that each mysterious letter corresponds to a material acceptance office allocated to the police. Many police units were equipped with proofed weapons for the army.

In parallel with this specific marking, an eagle/N, corresponding to the commercial test stamp, is found on the left side of the slide, the barrel, and the locking bolt.

Given that Mauser was the main supplier of the P.38 to the police forces (with very rare exceptions), the slide, frame, locking bolt, and barrel have the standard military inspection stamp (eagle/135, then eagle/WaA135).

It should be highlighted that, as a general rule, these police P.38s never have a letter after the serial number (which is found in the usual places: the left side of the slide, the frame, the barrel, and the last three figures on the locking bolt).

VARIANTS

On the basis once again of the markings and finish, a series of variants (and subvariants) concerning the P.38 assigned to the police can be singled out:

Design of the eagle/ WaA135 stamp

Detail of the markings present on the left side of a police "byf44." Note the absence of the letter level with the serial number and the presence of the eagle/N stamp.

1. Variant "byf"

This variant corresponds to the police P.38 bearing the codes "byf43" and "byf44."

When one looks more closely, a first subvariant comprising the "byf43" and "byf44" marked with an eagle/L can be distinguished. This production is counted at 4,600; the finish is bronzed.

The second subvariant (eagle/F) concerns only the "byf44" benefiting from a dual-tone finish. This represents a further 1,500 examples. It is possible that the P.38s with the code "byf44" were assembled in 1945, after their homologues "svw45." As has already been previously mentioned, this end-of-war period was a favorable environment for this type of assembly.

2. Variant "svw"

Only a small number of these P.38s seem to have been assembled, since the total production is estimated to be 300. It is therefore not necessary to specify that these police "svw45" are in the category of those P.38 that are the most difficult to acquire. The finish can be blued, dual tone, or even totally phosphate treated. Like some "byf44" already mentioned, they have the eagle/F stamp (on the right side of the slide).

3. Variant "ac"

To say the least, this third (and final) variant of the police P.38 does not shine with its enormous production figures. In fact, it is estimated that only 400 of these pistols were assembled. The stamp eagle/F (still present on the right side of the slide) faces a marking of the "ac43" or "ac44" type on two lines (in the usual position, on the left side of the slide). The morphology of the letters "ac" is different from that applied by the Walther factory. In this case, the letters "ac" are larger, in different characters, and situated above the year ("ac" over "43" or "44"). These slides come from the DWM Werk Lüttich. The three types of finish (blued, dual tone, or completely phosphate treated) all were used.

It is only the presence of specific markings that differentiates these pistols from their military counterparts. The slightest general finish of these weapons evolved in the same way between 1943 and 1945. The Bakelite grips were standard. Some magazines, accompanying essentially the "byf 43," nonetheless present the peculiarity of being numbered (the number of the weapon) on the forward part of the magazine bottom. It is likely that this numbering was applied after delivery of the weapon to the police unit. The systematic numbering of magazines ended at the beginning of 1942.

Faced with the relatively unobtrusive specific markings of these police P.38s, the collector must be very attentive: the stamps eagle/L and F can be almost imperceptible if a visual examination of a "byf 43" (or "44") or "svw45," or "ac43 "or "44," is undertaken too quickly. The owner of such a pistol should on the other hand consider themselves lucky, considering the relative scarcity of this type of weapon.

CHAPTER 7

P.38 MAGAZINES

It is a well-established fact that throughout the entire period of manufacture, the constituent parts of a magazine remained the same; the body of the magazine (or the frame), the spring, the magazine follower, the magazine bottom, and the magazine bottom latch were assembled in the same way. The differences were, on one hand, the level of finish, which was to follow a similar process (namely, a trend toward simplification), and, on the other hand, the markings. This magazine is made in steel and is designed for eight 9 mm Parabellum cartridges (or in very rare cases where the P.38 is chambered in 7.62 mm, .380, or .45). The left side of the frame presents seven small, round orifices that allow for a visual assessment of how full the magazine is. Each weapon is supplied with a spare magazine, which is kept in the holster.

It should be noted that the P.38 magazine was, in theory, also designed for other handguns made in large part from sheet metal (the Sheet metal P.38, for example). This was a case of

the vain attempts of the dying Third Reich to manufacture, cheaply and quickly, semiautomatic pistols with a simple level of operation.

The P.38 magazine is very easy to disassemble: First, press the small, round protuberance on the magazine bottom latch to move the magazine bottom forward. This maneuver frees the spring and the magazine follower. This disassembly is indispensable for a complete and effective cleaning of the magazine, as well as to examine for any possible military inspection stamps.

NUMBERING

Only the Walther firm numbered its P.38 magazines with the number of the weapon, and this was for a defined period.

The exact position of the number varied over time. Generally speaking, the following rules applied:

- For the zero series P.38 until the "ac" series without date, the number is found

The five components of a magazine: *top left*, magazine follower; *middle left*, the frame; *bottom left*, the magazine bottom; *bottom middle*, magazine bottom latch; *on the right*, the spring

Training in Brittany. Four German paratroops with General Bernard Ramcke (carrying a Walther PP). The first three paras are equipped with a P.08, carried on the right, and the fourth has a P.38 holster.

Numbering of a magazine on the bottom left side

Numbering of the magazines. *Left*: lengthwise marking at the rear of the magazine bottom. *Middle*: transversal marking on the front of the magazine bottom. *Right*: transversal (re) numbering made at an indeterminate date (larger-size figures).

Rare Magazine (P38v) with the ac code.

The practice of numbering the magazines disappeared in 1942; in other words, on the P.38 "ac42" from the end of group "c" and the beginning of group "d."

However, some P.38 magazines on later weapons are numbered ("ac44" for example), or on other manufacturers (e.g., "byf43" or "cyq"). In this case, several hypotheses have been put forward:

1. It was a postwar renumbering, by and for the ex–East German forces (P.38 of the Volkspolizei or VOPO), for example. But other origins of this renumbering can be considered.

2. The magazine bottom comes from another magazine (Salther) and has been remounted on a magazine frame bearing an eagle/135 (or an eagle/WaA135) or an eagle/88 stamp.

3. The magazine comes from a police P.38 ("byf43," for example). The German police had the habit of marking their magazines occasionally after reception. In view of the small number of P.38s assembled for the police, this hypothesis remains the most unlikely.

STAMPS ON THE P.38

The magazines assembled at Zella-Mehlis have the eagle/359 stamp; it was the number and their position that changed over time. Between 1939 and early 1942 (i.e., from zero series to the beginning of the "ac42" series), two stamps are counted[*] on the rear side of the magazine, either one next to the other in the lower part or at different levels (approximately $\frac{1}{5}$ and $\frac{4}{5}$). Likewise, all the other constituent parts (e.g., the magazine follower, the magazine bottom, and the magazine bottom latch) are tested apart from the spring, which could be weakened by such a marking. That means, therefore, as a general rule, that a numbered magazine from Walther magazines must possess a stamp (eagle/359) on the small parts, and two stamps (eagle/359) on the rear side of the form (up to the end of 1941 and early 1942).

The situation is simpler with magazines from Mauser factories, which have the eagle/135 (then the eagle/WaA135).

[*] Exception being the first P.38 of the zero series, which could show only one

at the base of the left side of the magazine body.

• For the P.38 "ac40" up to the "ac41," the serial number is localized crosswise on the forward part of the magazine bottom.

• For the P.38 "ac42," the serial number is on the magazine bottom, but it is positioned lengthwise on the rear part.

Unfortunately, this description does not take into consideration a certain superposition in the numbering system, since there are some P.38 "ac40" added to the "ac40" standard that have magazines presenting the same characteristics as those for the zero series P.38. The rules stated earlier must of course be interpreted with care, and it is indispensable to confer on them a certain flexibility.

The magazines of the first P.38s assembled by Mauser (code "byf42") possess two stamps of the eagle/135 on the rear side of the frame.

The existence of magazines bearing the "ac" code, the "du" code, or even a small "+" should be pointed out.

At the end of the conflict the WaffenAmt inspections were less frequent. That is why the many magazines of this period can be without these specific markings.

Concerning the "P.38" marking, it is noted that it is applied at the bottom of the left side of the magazine frame, near the serial number, from the end of the "ac" series without date. On rare occasions it is written on the right side of the frame. The majority of the P.38 magazines have this distinctive sign. But (authentic) magazines devoid of all markings can be found.

THE FINISH

The finish of the P.38 magazines was to follow a similar process to that of the pistols. A series of changes were carried out, with the objective of producing more and at a lower cost, while applying the modifications resulting from an ever more widespread use; at the end of 1944, therefore, two small ridges appeared on the upper side of the magazine follower (which was originally smooth). In addition, the magazine frame was closed by means of a series of stamping points, which are clearly visible on the left side.

The external appearance of these magazines also developed over time. The magazines accompanying the P.38s machined during the first years of manufacture are of an excellent quality. They are of a very uniform black-matte color and bear no traces of machining. Subsequently, little by little, the finish changed and traces of tool use became more and more visible; the bronzing became more and more superficial. It was replaced by a technique of phosphate coating that gave the metal its characteristic greenish coloration. These magazines are seen very frequently with weapons assembled in the last months of the war (P.38s "svw 45," "ac45," and other "cvq" codes prefixed "a" and "b," for example). Others did not have even the slightest protective finish and have the appearance of metal in its natural state.

It should be pointed out however that despite the unengaging appearance of these "end of war" magazines, all the manipulations inherent to their operation (i.e., loading of eight rounds, loading and unloading) took place without incident in the vast majority of cases. They remained perfectly interchangeable.

From left to right: two eagle/359 stamps on the bottom of the rear side, two eagle/359 stamps at different heights, and eagle/359 at the top; the eagle/WaA706 stamp accompanied by the code "jvd," two eagle/135 stamps situated at different heights, and eagle/135 stamp at the top

Comparison between an early magazine (1939) on the left and a later magazine (end of 1944 / early 1945) on the right

Comparison of magazine followers: *left*, smooth surface; *right*, ridged lengthwise

Details of the code "jvd" and the eagle/WaA706 inspection stamp from a magazine from the Erste Nordboehmische Metallwarenfabrik

Comparison of the different finishes: *left*, a magazine with a phosphate finish; *right*, a magazine with a blued finish

Capital letter "U" on the right and left sides of magazines with the code "jvd"

Detail of the P.38v marking

The P.38 on the front line

CODE "JVD"

This is the code of the Erste Nordboehmische Metallwarenfabrik, in occupied Czechoslovakia. The WaffenAmt assigned to this factory corresponded to the eagle/WaA706. Initially, these magazines equipped almost exclusively P.38s made by Spreewerke (code "cyq" or "cvq"). Toward the end of the war, starting at the end of 1944, they are also found on P.38s assembled by Walther (code "ac45" essentially). This "jvd" marking, alone or with the eagle/WaA706, can be found on different parts of the magazine: left, right, or rear side.

THE LETTERS "U" AND "V"

The capital letter "U" stands for the German word *Ungehartet*. This marking proves that the magazine has not been treated by tempering the steel. A text made this modification official in August 1944. This capital "U," which can be of varying sizes, is most often found on the lower part of the left side of the magazine frame (under the P.38 sign). But it is not unusual to find it on the right side of the frame.

The small letter "v" (*Veränderte Bauform*) corresponds to a modification of the dimensions of the metal sheet used to make the magazine. This letter, sometimes in a very small size, is always closely associated with the P.38 sign that was transformed into P.38v.

This modification was officially adopted in April 1944.

PRACTICAL ATTITUDE

The ideal concerning the P.38 is to own the original numbered magazine. This number must be situated in the suitable position, which varies depending on the period of its manufacture. These P.38s are not very frequent but are still encountered occasionally on the collectors' market or in private collections. The ultimate goal is to find a second magazine (reserve) also with the weapon number.

It should be acknowledged that this would be extremely rare. The collector has to settle for an honest (and elegant) compromise: to incorporate a magazine "compatible" with the period of manufacture of the pistol.

The same thing could be said about the later Walther P.38s, Spreewerke, and other Mausers. It is enough to simply ensure that the pistol has a magazine that is similar from the point of view of its finish and markings. The goal is to build the most homogeneous weapon possible, without allowing the search for an original magazine to become an obsession.

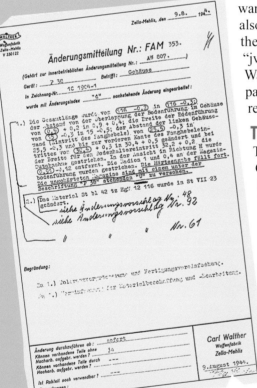

Reproduction of a document dated August 9, 1944, that makes official the use of the capital "U" on P.38 magazines

CHAPTER 8

AMMUNITION

I t is hardly necessary to introduce the 9 mm Parabellum cartridge. It was used throughout the world and indeed is still used in an impressive number of semiautomatic pistols and machine guns to this day.

The 9 mm Parabellum cartridge first appeared at the beginning of the twentieth century, at the same time as the birth of the Luger 1902 model.

Between 1908 and 1938, it was the P.08 chambered in 9 mm Parabellum (ordinary ball cartridge) that was used as a regulation handgun in the German army.

CARTRIDGE TYPES

1. Ordinary ball cartridge
This standard bullet is composed of a lead center surrounded by brass or nickel (later replaced by soft lead plated with copper). The case is rimmed and slightly tapered. The Berdan-type priming is placed in a crimped brass tip separated from the base of the cartridge by a line of black lacquer.

2. The m.E.: Pistolenpatronen 08 m.E. (mit Eisenkern) ball cartridge
In 1941, a cartridge with a new type of bullet was put into circulation. This projectile consisted of an iron core with a thin lead coat, surrounded by a soft, copper-plated iron. The bullet was then chemically blackened so as to be easily distinguished from the previous one. This practice was phased out at the end of 1944, at the time when these m.E cartridges were in the majority. They had a copper-colored

bullet plating. This bullet could be mounted on cases in brass or steel. During use, the steel cases manifested some flaws, such as fissures or breaks in the case. To remedy this, new steel cases, known as the first model, were developed. They had a reinforced base (i.e., thicker body and head) while keeping the two primer holes. They are referenced St+. This sign was from then on printed on the base of the cartridge and must, in theory, also be found on the label.

3. The S.E.: Pistolenpatronen 08 S.E. (mit Sintereisengeschoss)
Research was still ongoing to find lead substitutes, and a new projectile was developed and produced starting in 1942; this was a projectile composed of compressed iron filings, heated and concentrated by means of a binder (copper, among others). Unlike previous versions, it was not jacketed and is easily recognizable by its natural anthracite-gray color. This projectile is systematically mounted on first-model (St+) steel cartridges with reinforced base or on second-model cartridges. These new cartridges are characterized not only by the similar reinforcement of their body and base, but by the removal of one of the priming holes. The code assigned to these

Box of sixteen rounds dating from the end of the First World War

Left, a round-nose bullet; *right,* a bullet with flat-point round head

This adjutant of the 2nd Division Blindée is handling a superb captured P.38; he has attached a first-model holster to his belt.

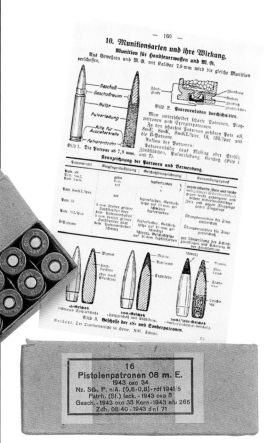

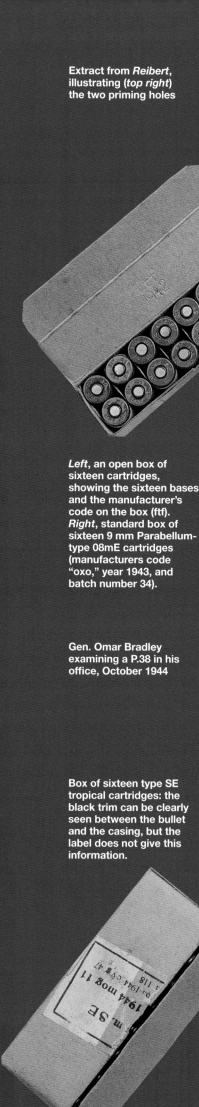

weapons fitted with a silencer, projectiles containing poison, training cartridges, inspection cartridges, helmet test cartridges, and so on.

THE BASE

The base of the 9 mm Parabellum cartridge presents a series of interesting inscriptions. The following can be distinguished on close examination:

- at 12 o'clock, the manufacturer's code

- At 3 o'clock, the features concerning the cartridge. A small, stylized star corresponding to a brass cartridge and the letters "St" indicate the presence of a cartridge in steel

- at 6 o'clock, the batch number, which should also be found on the fourth line of the label

- at 9 o'clock, the year of manufacture of the cartridge, abbreviated to the last two figures of the year in question

It should be noted that this order is not always respected by manufacturers.

The first code used on the bases was the letter "P" followed by one or more figures. This was used up to the beginning of the Second World War. Later, each manufacturer received a code name, made up of one to three minuscule letters. Approximately ninety such names directly concern ammunition manufacturers.

new cartridges is −St+. This is also meant to appear on the base of the cartridge and on the box label. It should be noted that these bullets had the unfortunate reputation of causing the rapid wear of the barrel.

4. Tropical cartridges

These are designed for use in hot and humid regions. A thin trim in black is applied at the seam between the bullet and the case; the primer benefits from the same treatment. This is designed to ensure a seal and prevent corrosion. This method also seems to concern ordinary cartridges such as the m.E and S.E. A special note, an abbreviation, is often stamped on the labels of boxes containing this type of ammunition: the letters "Tp" or "Trop" on the first line. But this marking is often lacking.

5. Other cartridge types

Apart from "standard" cartridge types, there is a series of ammunition reserved for very specific uses. Among these are the 9 mm Parabellum subsonic cartridges designed for

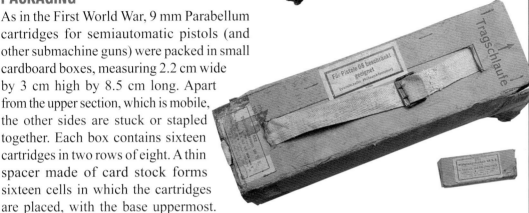

PACKAGING

As in the First World War, 9 mm Parabellum cartridges for semiautomatic pistols (and other submachine guns) were packed in small cardboard boxes, measuring 2.2 cm wide by 3 cm high by 8.5 cm long. Apart from the upper section, which is mobile, the other sides are stuck or stapled together. Each box contains sixteen cartridges in two rows of eight. A thin spacer made of card stock forms sixteen cells in which the cartridges are placed, with the base uppermost. Up until the beginning of the Second World War, these boxes also had small metal reinforcements on both ends of the base, and they also had a thin ribbon on the upper part. These boxes are light brown in color and very often have the manufacturers code and the abbreviated form of the date of manufacture. The most interesting part is, without doubt, the label on each box; the printed text contains complete and precise information concerning the type of cartridge in the box.

Fifty-two of these small boxes (of sixteen cartridges) are placed in a thick cardboard container. This measures approximately 31 cm high by 13 cm deep by 9 cm wide. At the bottom of the front side there is a label resembling the one on boxes of sixteen cartridges, which specifies the features of the ammunition present in the small boxes and also displays the total number of cartridges in the container (832). The container has a canvas strap (with a small metal buckle) to facilitate transport. These packs are identical to those for boxes for cartridges for type 98k rifles and light machine guns and Sturmgewehr.

For the next level, these packs are grouped by five in wooden boxes (Patronenkasten 88). Apart from the usual manufacturer's markings, the wooden box also has a larger label, giving the same information on the ammunition and also the number (4160). It weighs roughly 60 kilos.

THE LABEL

As mentioned earlier, the label on the box of sixteen cartridges (and also on larger containers) is a veritable gold mine of information. This rectangular paper label can cover the front side of the box or can be on three sides at once. The label has a light background, an inner black border, and a wide, blue central stripe.

Sometimes boxes are found that were clearly labeled twice. Generally speaking, on boxes produced before 1941, the inscriptions are written in Gothic script. Subsequently they used Latin characters. The text is printed in black ink.

In the vast majority of cases, the decoding of these labels is made easier if the following points of reference are borne in mind:

- First line: the number (16 Pistolenpatronen) and the type of cartridge (08 for the ordinary one, 08 m.E. or 08 S.E.)

- Second line: the year of manufacture, the manufacturer's code, and the batch number

- Third line: the type of powder (Nz. Stb.), the manufacturer's code, year, and batch

Reproduction of a label applied on the wooden case containing 4,160 cartridges in 9 mm Parabellum

The different elements of a sixteen-cartridge box (manufacturer's code "Kdg" and year 42), with its spacer and six green lacquer cartridges with blackened heads

The container of 832 cartridges with a series of labels and strap, with a small original box from the container next to it

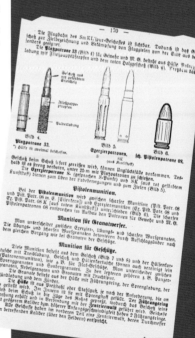

Extract from *Reibert*: next to the training cartridges for rifles, the representation of a 9 mm Parabellum cartridge

Left: "Tp" marking for tropical cartridges; *right*, "t" marking for Czechoslovakia

On the label, line 1: number and type of cartridges; *line 2*: year of manufacture, manufacturer's code, and batch number; *line 3*: features of the powder; *line 4*: features of the casing and projectile; *line 5*: characteristics of the core and the primer

Accompanied by a box from the First World War (*top right*), seven different boxes made during the Second World War, with the following codes: "dou," "dnh," "aux," "ak," "fb," "oxo"

- Fourth line: The type of casing (Pathr.) the year, the manufacturer's code, and the batch number. It is this batch number that must correspond to the number on the base of the cartridge.

- Fifth line: The type of projectile or bullet (Gesch.), the year, the manufacturer's code, and the batch number. The core (Kern) of the m.E. cartridges can also be detailed here.

- Sixth line: the type of primer (Zdh.), the year, the manufacturer's code, and the batch number

On a certain number of boxes, the figure "16" is alone and isolated at the top of the label (which corresponds, in a way, to the line zero). In the same way, the fourth and fifth lines mentioned above are sometimes regrouped on a single line.

On some boxes produced at the beginning of the conflict in the factories of occupied countries, a small letter is added at the end of the first line: a small "t" for Czechoslovakia and the letter "p" for Poland. It is known that great quantities of captured ammunition were put back into circulation for the German army in the original packaging.

The letters "Tp" or "Trop" can also appear at the end of the first line. This corresponds to the abbreviation of "tropical."

The very precise nature of these annotations does not prevent the occasional discovery of errors. In these cases, the contents do not always correspond to what is on the label (for example, label St, with base St+, etc.). The existence of such anomalies is not surprising considering the hundreds of millions of cartridges that were packed during the Second World War.

Only German ammunition benefited from such a luxury of information concerning the cartridges and their different components; this is far from the case for British or American ammunition.

CONCLUSION

The German 9 mm Parabellum cartridge alone represents a whole theme for collectors. Setting aside any possible legal difficulties concerning its possession, it should be recognized that it is often difficult to find these small boxes in a good state of preservation.

There seems to be a consensus to no longer use these (old) cartridges in modern or period firearms, but their age and irrefutable historical value should be taken into consideration. Some corrosion occurring inside the casing has been reported with cartridges that appear in good shape on the exterior. It must be remembered that this ammunition was designed to be used as quickly as possible and that manufacturers had not planned for or researched any possible use of these cartridges more than seventy years after they were made. This point also applies to other ammunition of the period, such as the 7.92 Mauser.

H. Dv. 254

Pistole 38

Beschreibung, Handhabungs-
und Behandlungsanleitung

Vom 1. 2. 40

Berlin 1940

Verlag von E. S. Mittler & Sohn

ACCESSORIES

THE LANYARD

This accessory seems to have been reserved initially for mounted troops. Later, its use spread to mechanized troops (motorcyclist and cyclist). All P.38s are equipped with a ring for the lanyard, situated on the lower left side of the grip. The left plate has a round or rectangular depression, depending on whether the plate is a fish scale plastic type or a standard ridged plate in Bakelite. This lanyard is made in canvas-type webbing with a closing system in leather, and the notation "P.38" is stamped here. The official documents mention that this lanyard can also be used with the P.08.

THE CLEANING KIT

The cleaning kit was officially adopted on September 4, 1934, and is abbreviated as R.G.34. It consists of a small metal box with rounded edges measuring 13.5 cm high by 8.5 cm wide by 2 cm deep. Divided into two compartments, it contains on one side a rag and on the other side a metal chain, two brushes, a buret of oil, and a small multipurpose tool. It was supplied from 1934 to all combatants equipped with a pistol, or a submachine gun, rifle, or machine gun. This kit is therefore not specific to any one weapon in particular and so was used by holders of a P.38. As a general rule it has markings specifying the name or the code of the manufacturer, the date of manufacture, and any military inspection stamps.

The R.G.34 is not an especially rare accessory, and it is not uncommon to come across them at military fairs. It completes any collection of German small arms very well.

P.38 instruction manual (dated February 1, 1940)

This sergeant (*fourth from the left in the foreground*) holds a P.38 with a sling in his left hand.

Detail of the closing mechanism of the lanyard

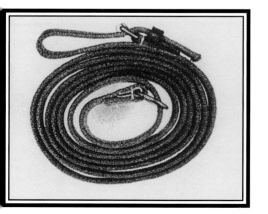

P.38 lanyard

Opposite page: Placed around a dual-tone P.38 on its left side (code "byf44"), the contents of an individual cleaning kit (the *reinigungsgerat* or RG34): two brushes, an oil buret in Bakelite, a metal chain, and a small multipurpose tool. There are also three magazines from three different manufacturers; *from left to right*, a Mauser-made phosphate-coated magazine, a bronzed Walther-made (sign P.38), and a bronzed example from the Erste Nordboehmische Metallwarenfabrik (code "jvd"). Three boxes of sixteen Pistolenpatronen 08 m.E. complete the group (code "aux," year 42 and two others: code "dnh," year 43).

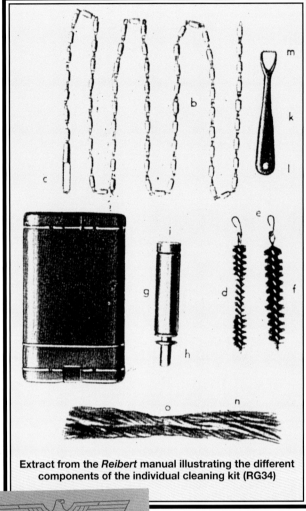

Extract from the *Reibert* manual illustrating the different components of the individual cleaning kit (RG34)

Different documents of the period: *left*, three pamphlets (dated 1941) of British origin on the P.38; *right*, a *Reibert* of the Wehrmacht dated 1943, containing a paragraph on the P.38

DOCUMENTS

Apart from the indispensable official manuals dedicated to the P.38, there are a series of regulation German works (in the style of *Reibert*) that mention this pistol in the section on handguns. These publications were often done a little after the official adoption. The collector has the opportunity of acquiring more specifically the editions destined for the different military service arms (e.g., Heer, Luftwaffe) and the police, for whom the P.38 was mentioned for the first time only in 1944.

In parallel, the Allies published a series of illustrated documents detailing the war hardware used by the German military. These publications review almost the totality of the enemy weapons, from the stick grenade to armored vehicles. They are meant, among other things, to facilitate the use of captured enemy weapons if the need came up, and of course the P.38 is referred to extensively. It is amusing to note that the English-language documents of this type dated at the end of 1941 discuss the P.08 extensively but make only a brief allusion to the P.38, about which there was not yet sufficient information. Another British publication of this time pointed out that the P.38 was probably the third most used in the German army (after the P.08 and the Mauser C96). The American secret service also published similar works. A copy of *German Infantry Weapons* dated May 25, 1943, accurately stated that the Pistole 38 became more frequently used in the German army and was replacing the Luger. This work specified on the same occasion that the P.38 did not possess the stopping power of the Colt M1911, but also that it was the only one to have double action. Knowledge of the characteristics of German war weapons became deeper over time, and the P.38 would no longer have any secrets for the victors.

CHAPTER 10

Observing through binoculars, giving a view of a first-model holster, the leather flap seems slightly shriveled.

Rear side of a first-model holster (code "hjg" and year 1941)

Rear side of a second-model holster (code "DLU" and year 1944)

Details of the markings on the rear side of a first-model holster: manufacturer's code "bdr," year marking with two figures (43), and the military inspection stamp

The holster for the P.38, like the majority of regulation holsters of this period, was made of leather (calfskin or pigskin; the latter is less supple). The color varied depending on the presentation, grade, or function of the owner (black or brown being the most widespread). This holster is worn suspended from the belt via two loops at the rear, on the left hip, with the butt facing the front. Normally the holster is rendered more solid by means of thick white stitching; however, some can have metal rivets, which reinforce the rear loops and the tab with the body of the case.

TYPES 1 AND 2

The collector who has the opportunity to find a complete set comprising a P.38, its original holster, and two magazines can consider themselves very lucky.

In theory, the following different official markings are found on the rear side:

- the P.38 sign

- the manufacturer's name or code

- the date of manufacture

- the WaffenAmt hallmark

Generally speaking, there are two main types of holster for the P.38:

FIRST-MODEL-TYPE HOLSTER (PISTOLENTASCHE 38 = HARD SHELL)

This was adopted on April 26, 1940 (in other words, at the same time as the weapon itself),

and was directly based on its illustrious forerunner, the P.08. It was characterized by its system of closing, which consisted of a leather flap that passed through a metal U-shaped ring, going from top to bottom. There is also an interior strap designed to facilitate the extraction of the pistol from its holster. It is manufactured in hardened leather and measures approximately 20 by 25 cm. Its general finish is usually excellent, and it protects the pistol in an optimal way. It has a side compartment to hold the reserve magazine. These holsters were assembled mostly between 1939 and 1943, but it is sometimes possible to find rarer examples dated 1944. For information purposes it should be mentioned that the case destined for the Cz 38 pistol—that is, the P39(t) in German classification—in 9 mm short caliber is virtually identical.

SECOND-MODEL-TYPE HOLSTER (PISTOLENTASCHE 38/1 = SOFT SHELL)

Even though this was assembled from 1943 onward, this second model case was not officially adopted until June 27, 1944. It resembles a smaller version of the Walther PP holster (it measures around 16 by 23 cm). It is mounted from a supple leather that can be smooth or slightly granular. Different types and qualities of leather have been used, and they were sometimes associated within one holster. The holster gives less coverage than its predecessor and therefore gives less protection. It does not have an interior strap. It still has a place for the second magazine, but this is found on the front side of the holster. The method of closing was simplified: it consisted of a tab that, from top to bottom, is housed in a metal button. There are, however, exceptions to this rule; different specimens assembled by certain manufacturers such as Gebr. Klinge at Dresdan-Lobtau (code "gxy") are provided with a flap that goes from bottom to top (without necessarily signifying a specific allocation to the police).

These second-model holsters were produced in a very large quantity in 1944 and to a lesser extent in 1945.

MARKINGS

1. The P.38 sign

The denomination of the pistol type is stamped in large print in the leather on the rear side of the holster. The sign measures approximately 3.6 by 1.7 cm, but these dimensions, along with the style of lettering, can vary to some extent. It is sometimes in an oval shape, and sometimes the "P" and the "38" are separated by a dot. This sign is designed to be more easily distinguishable from the P.08 holsters. The first ones conceived for the P.38 (dated 1939) did not have a distinctive sign, and there is clear evidence that this marking appeared some time in 1940.

2. The manufacturer's code or name

Until 1940–41, the manufacturer's name appeared in letters between the two rear loops on the holster. Occasionally, the commercial symbol was printed. Subsequently, it was a code that replaced the manufacturer's name, and this was to become more general for the majority of German military equipment. This operation seems designed to deceive foreign intelligence services regarding the exact origin of the material (for a while at least). Naturally, there are exceptions to this rule, in the form of later

A range of holsters: *top left*, first type; *top right*, police holster; *middle left*, holster with closing from bottom to top (code "GXY"); *right middle*, second type (standard); *bottom left*, second type of holster with smooth and embossed leather

An example of the personalization of a holster by its owner (manufacturer's code "hft" and year 42)

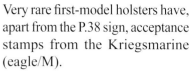

1) The commercial symbol (an oak leaf) of the Akah company

2) Year marking of one figure (year 1944, manufacturer's code "CXB")

3) Year marking of four figures (year 1943, manufacturer's code "gxy")

4) Example of a nine-figure contract number (on a leather belt)

5) Example of an ink marking on a second-model holster (manufacturer's code "DLU" and year 1945)

holsters still bearing the manufacturer's name (in '43 and '44).

3. The date of manufacture

It is closely associated with the name (then the code) of the manufacturer. It can have one, two, or four figures; for example:

figure "4" = year 1944
figure "42" = year 1942
figure "1945" = year 1945

The small number of P.38s assembled in 1939 and 1940 explains the fact that they are particularly difficult to find. There are of course exceptions to these rules in the form of undated holsters.

4. The WaffenAmt hallmark

This stamp represents the proof that the part is suitable for military use. It is found on the rear side of the holster. It should be highlighted that starting at the end of 1943, these inspections were carried out less regularly, meaning consequently that some authentic holsters (by definition the later ones) did not have WaffenAmt stamps.

5. Other markings

Some first- and second-model holsters sometimes have a series of nine figures stamped on the rear side, seemingly corresponding to a contract (or identification) number (e.g., 0/0655/0013). This type of numbering is found on other types of material such as bayonet holders and belts.

Note: The legibility of these different markings is sometimes very poor. The wearing away over time or the granular texture of the leather can sometimes seriously hinder the decoding process. The "denazification" also had the effect of causing the eradication of all representations of the swastika on a large number of holsters.

Very rare first-model holsters have, apart from the P.38 sign, acceptance stamps from the Kriegsmarine (eagle/M).

Less officially, it is possible to see the name of the owner of the weapon (and holster) written in white ink. The serial number of the pistol is also sometimes printed on the leather.

Some of these markings (WaffenAmt hallmark, manufacturer's code) are applied with the aid of an ink stamp. They are written inside the holster.

OTHER TYPES OF HOLSTERS

In addition to the most frequently used standard holsters, there were other types for a P.38:

1. Ersatz models were assembled at the end of the war from very diverse material. At the same period, the Germans developed the concept of a multipurpose holster; these were designed for different handguns of similar dimensions.

2. Numerous eyewitness accounts state that some P.38s were captured in P.08 holsters. The P.38 has plenty of room but is well protected. Concerning the reserve magazine, that was another matter entirely. This problem was sometimes resolved by cutting the holder for the magazine. In the same way, holsters designed for the FN Browning 35 model Nazi—that is, the P640(b) in German classification—also seem to have been diverted from their original destination. These holsters very closely resemble the second-model holsters described earlier. The differences include the closing (from the bottom to the top), rear loops (only one and wider), and the size of the housing for the reserve magazine (wider so as to accommodate the thirteen-round magazine). A P640(b) holster that held a P.38 is recognizable by the friction traces on the inside and mainly by the abnormal extension of the orifice at the end of the closing tab.

3. Theuermann-type holsters (Theuermann patent no. 695930) also seem to have been

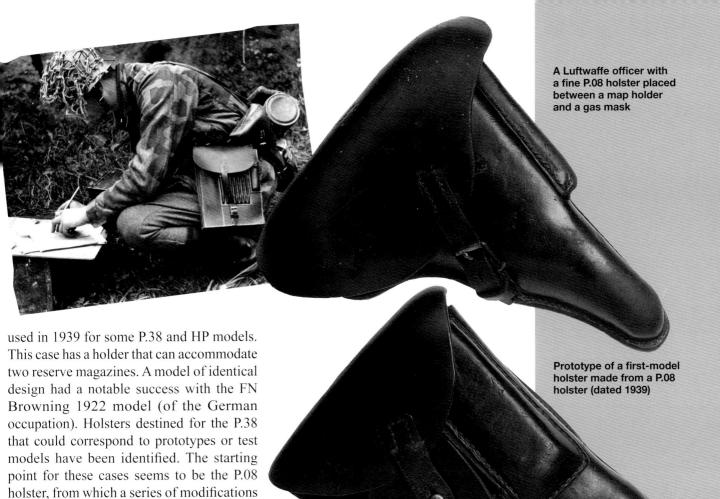

A Luftwaffe officer with a fine P.08 holster placed between a map holder and a gas mask

used in 1939 for some P.38 and HP models. This case has a holder that can accommodate two reserve magazines. A model of identical design had a notable success with the FN Browning 1922 model (of the German occupation). Holsters destined for the P.38 that could correspond to prototypes or test models have been identified. The starting point for these cases seems to be the P.08 holster, from which a series of modifications were made.

Similarly, there are first-model holsters that have been transformed into second-model holsters.

4. Many captured holsters were personalized by their new owners. Very often, the surname or first name, the address, the rank, or a key date were engraved. Other Allied combatants inserted metal badges taken from German uniforms in the leather of their holster. On a more practical note, GIs would sometimes have to insert a metallic piece between the rear loops of the case in order to be able to hang it from the US regulation belt.

5. Troops of the Italian Social Republic (the RSI, the forces that remained faithful to Mussolini after the armistice of September 8, 1943) were also intensive users of the P.38. The holsters used by the Italians come either from German stocks (cases of the first or, more generally, the second model) or were manufactured by the Italians themselves. These holsters were either fairly standard or more "traditional," with cuts that gave them a more minimalist appearance.

6. Shoulder holsters for the P.38—and, by extension, for other handguns such as the P.08, the Walther PP, and the P35(p)—have been much written about. It is accepted that

Prototype of a first-model holster made from a P.08 holster (dated 1939)

Transitional-type holster: this is a first-model holster transformed by means of a series of cuts into a second-model holster.

these holsters were never officially adopted by (or supplied to) troops in uniform (and this included aircrews and armored-vehicle crew, who would have been the most likely to benefit).

It is nonetheless probable that they were both tested and used by members of the secret service and by civilian personnel authorized to carry a weapon. Some holsters of this type were, however, acquired by the combatant on an individual basis. American authors concur that the majority of shoulder holsters present on the market were assembled for US troops just after the end of the Second World War. Many "standard" holsters would have been transformed into shoulder holsters. The presence or absence of specific markings (WaffenAmt, date, name, or manufacturer's code stamps) does not clarify the situation. It should be admitted that there is no photographic proof, nor are there any official administrative records of this very particular type of holster being used by troops.

P.38 POLICE HOLSTER

Holsters for the P.38 police have a certain number of particularities. The first is their rarity; they were made in a small quantity

Example of the use of a small metallic part indicating that a German holster can be suspended from a US regulation belt

Kepi eagle inserted in the leather of a captured handgun holster

February–March 1944. Prince Borghese, commander of the Decima Flottiglia MAS, with his P.38 in the most simplified holster, composed of a single strap.

only during a relatively short period from early 1943 to early 1945. These first-model holsters were assembled mostly in Berlin. Two manufacturers' names appear systematically in this context: Otto Sindel for the year 1943, and A. Fischer for the year 1944.

Apart from the name and the location of the manufacturer, the eagle/B-type police acceptance stamp is also found on the rear side of the holster. The serial number of the pistol can also be stamped in the leather, which was common practice in the German police. The P.38 sign is in the usual place.

The system of closing these cases is also different from those destined for the Wehrmacht. For the police holster, a leather tab affixes to a metal button after going through a loop (in leather), from the bottom to the top.

Another controversy exists concerning the authenticity of second-model holsters that were specifically assigned to the police. These holsters surfaced at the beginning of the 1990s in parallel with the disappearance of the Eastern Bloc. Ukraine is often cited as the "country of origin" of these holsters. They are characterized by the presence of a stylized eagle similar to the one printed on the first-model holsters, but lacking the letter "B" (a serious problem!). In addition, they close from top to bottom. The leather used can be a smooth or grainy texture. The question concerning their allocation to the police forces of the Third Reich is still not resolved, and one should therefore be wary.

It is important however to underscore the fact that a second-model holster that closes from bottom to top does not necessarily make it a police holster.

REPRODUCTIONS

P.38 holsters cannot be discussed without mentioning the problem of reproductions, which have been in circulation for a number of years on the collectors' market.

The collector must therefore be extremely vigilant before acquiring this type of material. There are fortunately a series of small indications that could prove to be useful.

It is important to be wary of holsters that are too new. Some absolutely new second-model P.38 holsters were found a few years ago in Ukraine and then imported to the United States. The flap had never even been folded up! Conversely, some were aged artificially by skillful forgers.

The characteristic odor given off by new leather should be trusted to detect a copy.

The presence (or absence) of Nazi markings does not have any bearing on the authenticity of the piece. Some authentic holsters have no markings, whereas some fakes have too many! Sometimes, cases of the period can be seen where one or more stamps have been added to make it "more authentic." These same stamps were added on holsters used by the armed forces of the former East Germany. The task of the amateur is therefore complicated when it is known that a good number of these holsters were assembled according to identical plans and with the same raw materials as their Nazi counterparts. It goes without saying that the stamps applied with ink are also a concern regarding this issue.

The general finish of the case is worthy of attentive study by the collector. The copy generally has a cruder finish, with thicker leather and irregular cuts. Some copies can be identified extremely easily.

The inside of a used period holster always has friction traces at locations where the weapon has been moved in and out of the case. The pressure zones between the case and the hammer (or the sights) appear in the form of black marks.

To summarize, in a field as dangerous as that of German Second World War militaria, great care should be taken. To avoid disappointment, you should first carry out the maximum amount of research, and second, you should handle, examine, and even "smell" a great number of holsters to build up your own experience.

Details of the markings on a rare P.38 police holster: the name of the manufacturer (Otto Sindel), the place of manufacture (Berlin), the date of manufacture (1943), the specific eagle/B stamp, and the P.38 sign are visible.

CHAPTER 11
RARITIES

A postwar training P.38

A POLICE SPREEWERKE

Specialist American literature points out the existence of a P.38 made by Spreewerke (code "cyq," serial number 9920k) bearing a specific eagle/L-type marking, situated on the right side of breech block.

The weapon in question was documented a few years ago in South Africa, indicating that it is probably not a fake, given the weak local interest in this type of item.

It is the only P.38 reported in this way. It should be kept in mind that Mauser remained the main supplier to the German police both during and after the Second World War.

A NAVAL P.38

In the United States, a P.38 also from the Spreewerke workshops was identified with markings of the Kriegsmarine. This P.38, bearing the serial number 4354u, has a small eagle-type (swastika) stamp, MIII/3, on the forward part of the trigger guard on the left side. The pistol has no other particularity.

Another "cyq" was identified with a pair of anchors (of the German navy) on the left side of the slide (serial number 5435g).

It should be remembered that the Kriegsmarine was equipped with a certain number of P.38s, but the vast majority of them did not have distinctive stamps. It is estimated that only twenty-five P.38s had specific Kriegsmarine markings.

THE HP USTASHIS

A pro-Nazi fascist regime controlled the Croatia of the period. In this particular political context, Germany supplied a small number of weapons to its ally—among them, some beautifully finished Walther PPs. The serial numbers are between 12311 and 12570.

They are easily recognizable by the small logo present on the right side of the breech block. This represents the Ustashi emblem (the crest). Some P.08s, also delivered to the Croats, have the same type of marking. Many of these pistols in the hands of the Croat Waffen-SS disappeared in the mud and ice of the eastern front.

THE SWEDISH HP

In 1939 and early 1940, the Walther firm delivered a small quantity of HP models to the Swedish state (Pist. M/39). As with all model P.38s and other HP assembled at that time, these weapons present a remarkable degree of finish. They display "fish scale"-type plastic grip plates and still have a rectangular section firing pin. Crown/N-type commercial stamps are also found along with some rare eagle/359-type stamps.

Their principal characteristic is a capital letter "H" (applied, in all likelihood, by the Walther firm), which precedes the serial number. This is on the right side of the frame, level with the forward part of the trigger guard. The Walther banner and the HP logo are on the left side of the slide. The serial numbers range between H1001 and H2065. It should be noted that the Swedes sometimes applied unit markings on the right side of the frame.

A schematic presentation of the police eagle/L

Representation of the marking of the German navy

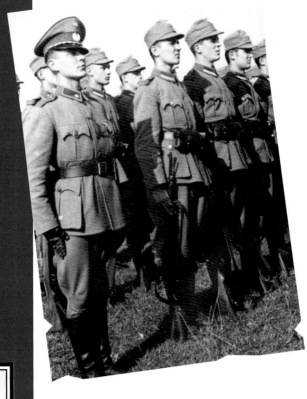

Stamp representing the Ustashi emblem

Details of a postwar training P.38

This small contract (around 1,000 specimens) ended at the beginning of the Second World War.

TRAINING MODELS

There are only three or four known authentic training P.38s dating from the Nazi period. The majority of them are now in American collections. As with all training pistols, these were destined to be used either within the factory itself or in training centers (or other arsenals).

The Walther banner is found on the majority of training P.38s along with a part of the indication (of the HP). In addition, these pistols have a serial number that is not part of an existing series but instead seems to reflect an internal number. Triangular markings with sides several millimeters in length are stamped on the slide. Some other training weapons assembled by Walther present the same feature. They are also found on the base of some ammunition known as dummy cartridge (20 mm, for example).

The amateur collector of this type of pistol can always make do with the postwar training P.38 coming from the Ulm arsenal (town situated in the former Federal Republic of Germany), where the P.38 was again made for the Bundeswehr (starting in 1957).

THE P.38 WITH SILENCER

Very little is known about the P.38 with a special barrel enabling the addition of a silencer. American documentation identified the existence of a "byf 44" (serial number 2532t) that appears to have benefited from this feature.

Care should be taken concerning possible modifications carried out postwar by "enthusiastic handymen," who transformed ordinary P.38s into extremely rare P.38s accompanied by silencers.

THE "DOV" CODE

The debate concerning these P.38s marked "dov" began in 1972, when a ten-page article was published in a German-language review (*Waffen-Revue* 7:1055). Contained in the article was the reproduction of a drawing of a letter "P" with the code "dov" on the left side of the slide. This code corresponds in fact to a branch of the Brno arsenal situated at Vsetin in Czechoslovakia. Some 98k rifles assembled in 1945 and 1946 by the Czechs have this famous code. As far as can be ascertained, these rare surviving pistols correspond to reassemblies carried out from diverse origins (dating from the war and postwar periods). They were rebronzed and renumbered, sometimes in the context of being used by the Volkspolizei, or by the Austrian army. Furthermore, in 1946, an expert in American military light weapons mentioned the existence of P.38s with the code "dou" in a report. It is highly likely that the "v" was taken for a "u," but it is difficult to imagine that the code was confused with the "byf" or "cyq" code.

Nevertheless, a further point remains unanswered: nothing is known about the origin of the machine tools that could have been used in this new assembly line.

It can be imagined that these machine tools were provided with a view to production, and there is even the daring hypothesis stating that the material taken from the FN at the beginning of September 1944 was used for that purpose. It is pure conjecture since there is no concrete proof. Code "dov": myth or reality?

SEVERAL FAKES AMONG MANY
A Model SA der NSDAP

This is a P.38 "ac41" (serial number 7514f) on which a well-equipped forger applied the following markings: the logo of the SA on the left side of the slide, level with the safety lever, and a marking of the SA type "der Gruppe Berlin-Brandenburg" on the forward part of the grip. The deception was exposed after this "unique" piece was offered for sale in the United States at the beginning of the 1980s. It had been identified in a database several years earlier, devoid of any supplementary markings! The existence of a Mauser-made P.08 was also pointed out (code "S42"), dated 1938 and bearing the same type of markings.

A Fake Police P.38

It seems that other forgers (or perhaps the same) took on the domain of police P.38. A military P.38 with the code "svw45" was modified and transformed into an "ultrarare" police "svw45" (production estimated at 300 specimens) via the addition of an eagle/F on the right side of the slide.

OTHER UNCLASSIFIABLE RARITIES

In this category, the following P.38 can be included:

1. P.38s in 7.65 mm and 22 Long rifle calibers, enlivened according to the will (and the budget) of the sponsor, with finely worked wooden grips and other distinctive features

2. P.38s with lightened frames in aluminum. The bronzing applied therefore has a different coloring, tending to be more matte.

3. Experimental P.38s (or prototypes) present an incomplete finish (unblued components), having neither legend nor serial number nor even the very small numbers (001, 002, etc.).

The collector confronted with this very distinctive type of P.38 must use all his critical faculties to acquire the "rare bird."

P.38 equipped with a silencer

Ideally, the maximum information on the history of the weapon should be obtained; the owner is sometimes the very person to provide vital information on this subject. In the vast majority of cases, however, the small/large? number of owners means that reliable information is not easy to get. The certificate of captured enemy equipment, drawn up by American military authorities when the US combatant returned to his country, sometimes still with his pistol, noted the name of the user and the serial number of the weapon and the date of declaration. This type of document proves to be very useful when you are judging the origin of the weapon.

Next, the weapon must be thoroughly examined, and attention should be focused on markings and bronzing. A stamp can be restruck, removed, or added, all of which can leave traces. The pistol (or some of its components) can also have been subject to re-bronzing after the war in military arsenals or even in a "collector's" backroom.

These markings, distinctive signs, and other serial numbers must then be compared with information in specialized documentation.

The opinion of the specialist can also be extremely important in these circumstances; it should be remembered that the skill of the forger is such that anyone can be deceived. If you are in doubt, it is best to refrain from buying.

SA sign applied on a fake

CHAPTER 12

OTHER MARKINGS

BH marking

35 stamp

Durofoe marking

ING marking

Privat marking

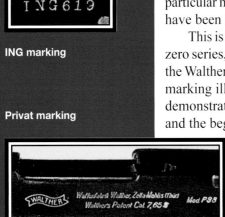

BH MARKING

This marking, flanked by a two-headed eagle, is applied on the left side of the frame level with the trigger guard on a certain number of P.38s. It proves the use of these pistols by the Austrian army (Austrian Bundesheer) after the Second World War. It seems that France supplied the Austrian army and police with some of these P.38s at the end of the 1950s. For the most part, these pistols preserve their original finish but can nonetheless have been subject to rebronzing; however, it seems that all the firing pins were replaced.

HEGE MARKING

This was the marking of Georg Hebsacker, a merchant from the former West Germany. These markings are found on other weapons such as Femaru and Tokagypt pistols that were traded by this wholesaler.

THE DUROFOE MARKING

This marking, found on the inside of the grips of some P.38s assembled at the end of the war (in particular the "ac45"), corresponds to the identity of the manufacturer. It is occasionally seen on plastic handguards on G43 rifles.

THE PRIVAT MARKING

A small number of P.38s having this very particular marking on the left side of the frame have been identified.

This is essentially on early pistols (mainly zero series, HP models, and other 480s) from the Walther firm workshops. It seems that this marking illustrates a use of the weapon as a demonstration piece at the end of the thirties and the beginning of the forties.

THE FIGURE 35

This figure is sometimes found on various parts (e.g., barrel, frame) on P.38s made by the Walther firm. Its significance is still unknown. It would have been applied fairly early on in the assembly process, and in any case before bronzing. This figure is seen on both the first HP models as well as on the later "ac45."

THE ING MARKING (FOLLOWED BY A NUMBER)

This is a marking applied by the Michigan state police. In theory it was reserved for weapons with no serial number.

THE FRENCH STAR

It is fairly easy to notice this marking on the right side of the slide of P.38s assembled under the control of the French forces. The P.38 does not have exclusivity on this small, five-pointed star, since it is found on P.08s and 98k carbines assembled for the French armed forces in the period immediately after the war. Many hypotheses have been formulated, but the most commonly accepted one is that the French selected a stamp that was not yet in use, and then applied it on weapons as a final acceptance stamp. In any case, it is very practical to differentiate the P.38 "svw45," "svw46," and "byf44" assembled under the aegis of the French control commission for Nazi P.38 production.

MARKINGS OF THE FORMER EASTERN BLOC

Despite the former Eastern Bloc being outside the scope of this book, it is useful to be able to discern the specific markings applied after the war by the armed forces of the former East Germany (and to a lesser extent Czechoslovakia).

In this context, it is necessary to differentiate the crown/N, the crown/U, the crown/R, the Suhl eagle, the unit markings of the Vopos in a "sun," the type 2/1001 markings, and the transformation work date code. These weapons have very often been completely rebronzed and have sometimes been subject to other more-extensive mechanical modifications (e.g., change of barrel).

THE RW MARKING

This marking probably corresponds to an inspection mark proving that the weapon had undergone a review in an arsenal. It is also found on some P.08s, which is not surprising given the fact that it seems to have been specifically used by the Mauser company.

THE "MYSTERIOUS" ASTERISK

The meaning of this small mark remains unknown. One of the most fashionable theories attempts to prove that this asterisk corresponds to evidence that a strength test had been carried out. Others see here more of a final "reinspection" trace after repair or adjustment by the manufacturer. Whatever the case, it concerns the three manufacturers of the P.38. It is also seen on bayonets and barrels on 98k rifles, FN 10/22 pistols (of the occupation), P.08s, and G43s. As far as the P.38 is concerned, it seems more frequently applied on specimens bearing the "cyq" (and "cvq") code.

FOREIGN TEST STAMPS

Depending on the legislation in effect in the country, some P.38s had to undergo a new test when they were acquired. The principle is absolutely identical to that applied at the time of a P.38's conception. At the shooting range, the weapon was tested with the aid of a cartridge with a greater amount of powder compared to standard ammunition. Later, the pistol was marked in various places with official stamps (Liege testing stand, British Neutralization Process). These markings can occasionally be a nuisance for the collector looking for an original piece in its "pure state." The proofing, however, is reassuring for the regular shooter.

Other stamps are added when the weapon is neutralized (e.g., the French-crowned "AN," for Arme Neutralisée: deactivation proof logo). Applying different technical methods, which vary according to the country, inspectors render the weapon as definitively unfit for firing. The acceptance of this neutralization constitutes however (the author's point of view) a major concession on the part of the collector. A real collector/owner status means that such catastrophes can be avoided.

Right side of a "svw45" with a small, five-pointed star

This French parachutist in Indochina is holding a P.38 in his right hand; the leather holster on his right hip can also be seen.

Stamps of the Liege testing stand (Belgium) on a P.38 barrel

British stamps (BNP) on a P.38 barrel

CONCLUSION

One of the attractions of a P.38 collection is that it can have different identities. The "super general" collector is content with just one piece, taking the time to select a fine example to which he or she adds a holster corresponding to the year, a spare magazine, and even one or more period cartridge boxes. Other "giants" of this period that could accompany a P.38 include the indispensable P.08, the robust American Colt M1911A1, and the trusty British Enfield revolver, all of which particularly come to mind.

The "general" collector, however, can make do with three P.38s, besides a Walther also including a Spreewerke (code "cyq") and a Mauser (code "byf"). The accessories mentioned above complete this group harmoniously, but other variations on the theme of the P.38 can also be envisaged.

The collector can take an interest in a single manufacturer, in that case taking a particular interest in P.38s from Walther company workshops and, in parallel, other handguns from the same maker (Walther PP, PPK, or flare pistols).

The code of the P.38 also presents a potential source of research. The code "byf," for example, exists on other German weapons of this period.

A specific year (or other time period) also constitutes a possible approach, with one collector being attracted by the Walther pre-1942 range and another focusing more on end-of-war weapons.

The post–Second World War P.38 (deliberately not discussed in this special edition) can also be an attractive domain for the collector.

This postwar period can be approached either by continuing on from the P.38 of the Second World War (the "byf 44" and other Nazi "svw 45" taking over from their French

German parachutists in Tunisia. The soldier on the left has an MG42 and a P.38 (first-model holster).

"counterparts") or in an isolated manner (Walther P1, P4, P.38K, commemorative, and other Manhurin).

The collector of German police weapons must possess a P.38 belonging to this organization. A "byf 43" or "44" with an eagle/L or eagle/F stamp would be a fine accompaniment to a P.08 with a Mauser banner or a (police) Sauer & Sohn. The search for a specific police P.38 holster also falls within this context.

The foreign stamps can also be the starting point for a very original collection: a P.38 bearing a Czech barrel (code "fnh"), a slide from the FN (eagle/WaA140) of a frame marked BH (illustrating an Austrian use), or even a small, five-pointed star (proof of use by the French army).

Some fortunate—and above all, lucky—collectors will be able to turn toward the experimental models (or prototypes) of the model MP types, such as MP, AP, and other Walther zero series models. P.38s made in another caliber such as the 9 mm Parabellum (22 LR cal., 7.65 mm cal.) can also fall into this same category.

But it should be pointed out that the very rare parts of this type offered for sale reach astronomical prices, capable of discouraging a good number of collectors.

The former Eastern Bloc also offers a rich theme. P.38s assembled by the Czechs in the immediate postwar period can also enter into this category.

Last, if the excessiveness does not frighten you, it is possible to imitate the American collector who brought together no fewer than 245 P.38s; in other words, an example of all the P.38s made by the three contractors—indexed by letter, corresponding, for example, to an "ac41" without letter, followed by an "ac41" with a (small) letter "a," then by the letter "b" and so on, and then the same thing for the "byf" and "cyq." This award-winning collection is frequently displayed in the United States.

These different possibilities are of course given as guidelines only. Each collector must create a collection in relation to availability and his or her personal ambitions and financial means, and not forgetting a little bit of luck.

An unorthodox way of carrying a P.38

BIBLIOGRAPHY

BOOKS

Buxton, Warren H. *The P.38 Pistol*. Los Alamos, NM: U. C. Ross Books, 1978.

Gangarosa, Gene, Jr. *P.38 Automatic Pistol: The First Fifty Years*. South Hackensack, NJ: Stoeger, 1993.

Hoffschmidt, E. J. *Know Your Walther P.38 Pistols*. Stamford, CT: Blacksmith, 1974.

Malherbe, Michel. *Le P.38 seigneur de la guerre*. Vernueil-sur-Avre, France: Crépin Leblond, 1994.

Malherbe, Michel. *Les pistolets allemands, 1914–1945*. Puiseaux, France: Edition Pardès, 1993.

Rankin, James L. *Walther*. Vol. 1, *Models PP and PPK, 1929–1945*. Coral Gables, FL: J. L. Rankin, 1974.

Rankin, James L. *Walther*. Vol. 3, *Pistolen, 1908–1983*. Coral Gables, FL: J. L. Rankin, 1981.

Still, Jan C. *Axis Pistols: World War Two 50-Year Commemorative Issue*. Douglas, AK: J. C. Still, 1989.

Still, Jan C. *Third Reich Lugers and Their Accessories*. Douglas, AK: J. C. Still, 1988.

Whittington, Robert B., III. *German Pistols and Holsters, 1934–1945: Military, Police, NSDAP*. 4 vols. Hooks, TX: Brownlee Books, 1969.

MAGAZINES

Automag. Monthly review for members of National Automatic Pistol Collector Association (NAPCA).

La Gazette des Armes.

THANKS

J. P. Chantrain
D. Cornet
A. Krutzek
G. Machtelinckx
A. Nowak
A. Van Lancker
J. L. Visée

All color photographs are courtesy of Marc de Fromont, unless otherwise noted.